THE 24/7 Manifestation Method

LATHA JAY

THE 24/7 Manifestation Method

BECOMING A MAGNET FOR SUCCESS IN JUST SEVEN DAYS

WILEY

Published by John Wiley & Sons, Inc., Hoboken, New Jersey.

Library of Congress Cataloging-in-Publication Data has been applied for:

Cloth: 9781394424115
ePub: 9781394424122
ePdf: 9781394424139

Cover Design: Wiley / Paul McCarthy
Cover Art: © Lumata / Shutterstock

Printed and bound by CPI Group (UK) Ltd, Croydon, CR0 4YY

C9781394424115_200826

For the woman who knows she is meant for more…

May you stop waiting

and start becoming.

And to my A-Team,

Amma, Adam, Avani, Aru, and Ayli,

you are my greatest manifestation

and my reason for becoming her.

Contents

Introduction: You Are Not Here by Accident

If you are holding this book, reading these words, or even just feeling pulled toward something more … I want you to know this: you are not here by accident.

There is a version of your life that you can already feel. Not logically. Not on paper. But somewhere deeper. A version of you that feels more aligned. More expressed. More certain. And more like you.

And yet, if you are anything like most people I have worked with, taught, or simply been human alongside, you may have also felt the gap. The gap between what you want and what you're experiencing. The gap between who you know you could be and who you are being on a daily basis.

And that gap can be frustrating.

Because it is not that you do not want it badly enough. It is not that you are not capable. It is not even that you do not believe in manifestation. It is that you have likely been taught manifestation in a way that is incomplete.

You have been told to visualize. To affirm. To think positively, good vibes only. To "act as if."

And while those things are not wrong, they are absolutely not the full picture. Because manifestation is not something you do once a day.

It is something you are doing **all day**.

Every thought.

Every reaction.

Every decision.

Every belief you reinforce.

Every time you say yes when you mean no.

Every time you shrink, avoid, overthink, or play small.

You Are Always Manifesting

Not just when you sit down with a journal. Not just when you light a candle. Not just when you remember to "get into alignment." But in the middle of your real life. Your conversations. Your habits. Your patterns. Your triggers. Your choices.

That is where your results are actually created.

And that is why so many people feel like manifestation "works sometimes" but not consistently. They are practicing it occasionally, but living in contradiction the rest of the time.

This book was written to change that.

I did not write this book to give you another set of techniques that you will try for a few days and then forget. I wrote this book to give you a way of living. A way of thinking, responding, and being. A way that turns manifestation from something you try into something you embody.

Over the years, through my own life, my personal transformations, and the work I have done with thousands of women during retreats, programs, and real conversations, I started to notice a pattern. The people who created real, lasting change were not the ones who knew the most techniques. They were the ones who were consistent in who they were being.

They learned how to align their mindset, their emotions, their identity, and their actions, not just in moments of motivation, but in their everyday lives. They stopped "doing manifestation" and started living in a way that naturally produced the results they desired.

That is what this book is about.

Inside these pages, I am going to introduce you to something I call the **24/7 Manifestation Method** because your life is not created in isolated moments. It is created in patterns. And when you learn how to shift those patterns, everything changes.

This book will walk you through a simple, structured, and powerful way to do exactly that. You will learn how to

understand what is actually creating your current reality,

identify the patterns that are keeping you stuck,

shift your internal state in real time,

align your thoughts, emotions, identity, and actions, and

begin showing up as the version of you who already has what you desire.

This is not about becoming someone else. It is about embodying who you have always been, without the layers of fear, conditioning, and self-sabotage.

This book is for the woman who knows she is meant for more. The one who feels it. Even if she cannot fully explain it yet. The one who is tired of starting over. Tired of getting excited and then falling back into old patterns. Tired of knowing what to do but not doing it consistently. The one who is ready to stop waiting.

And ready to start becoming.

As you move through this book, I want you to read it differently. Not just as information but as an invitation. An invitation to notice yourself and to observe your patterns. An invitation to interrupt what no longer serves you and to choose differently, again and again.

You do not need to do this perfectly. You just need to stay present long enough to begin. The moment you start living in alignment, even slightly, your reality begins to respond. And once you see that, you cannot unsee it.

This is where it begins.

PART I

The Reasoning Behind the 24/7 Manifestation Method

CHAPTER 1

Your Thoughts Create Your Reality (But That's Not Enough)

If your life were a playlist, what track would it be looping right now?

Love songs and green-light anthems, or background noise that keeps repeating the same old verse?

I want you to sit with that for a second, because it tells the truth in a way your mind sometimes refuses to.

Your life has a soundtrack. Your nervous system has a soundtrack. Your inner dialogue definitely has a soundtrack. And whether you realize it or not, you replay the same emotional tracks all day long. Some people live in a loop of "I'm safe, I'm supported, I can handle this." Other people are on "Brace yourself. Something's about to go wrong. Don't get too excited."

We don't just live in circumstances. We live in states.

And here is the quiet truth your life keeps whispering, even when you're too busy to hear it: Your inner world creates your outer world.

Every thought you think, every emotion you carry, every belief you repeat, none of it is neutral. These are not invisible experiences happening only inside your head. They are energetic signals rippling outward into the field around you. You are broadcasting a frequency all day long, whether you are aware of it or not.

Reality is simply the echo.

If you have ever walked into a room and immediately felt tension before anyone spoke, that was frequency. If you have met someone whose presence felt calming, magnetic, or grounding without them "doing" anything at all, that was frequency too. Everything about you—your breath, posture, tone, microreactions, and inner dialogue—is energy in motion.

The universe does not respond to what you want. It responds to what you are. But here is the catch and the reason so many manifestation methods fall flat: Thoughts alone will not get you to the life you want.

You can think "I'm abundant" 20 times a day while your body tightens when you check your bank account and your daily choices whisper, "I don't trust myself." You can say "I'm open to love" while bracing every time someone gets close. You can visualize success while your nervous system is still operating from fear. Your nervous system processes information faster than your conscious mind. Before a thought ever becomes a belief, your body has already decided whether something feels safe.

That is not alignment. That is mixed messaging.

Manifestation is not a slogan or a wish list. It is not positive thinking or hoping hard enough. Manifestation is a state of aligned energetic being, a harmony between your thoughts, your emotions, your identity, and your actions. When those four elements begin vibrating together, your life starts to hum like a perfectly tuned instrument. That coherence is what makes your reality respond.

This chapter is where that harmony begins. Before we go any further, we need to talk about why effort alone has never been enough. Not as a philosophy, but as a lived practice. Not as inspiration you forget by Tuesday, but as a way of relating to yourself that changes the rest of your life. If effort were the answer, you would already be living the life you want.

You have tried. You have pushed. You have set intentions, made plans, started over, and told yourself, "This time will be different."

And for a moment, it usually is. Until it isn't.

Until something pulls you back into the same patterns. The same thoughts. The same emotional reactions. The same behaviors that quietly recreate the reality you were trying to leave behind.

This chapter is not here to motivate you to try harder.

It is here to show you why trying harder has not worked … and what actually does. Inside this chapter, we are going to slow everything down and look at manifestation differently than you may have ever been taught.

We are going to explore

- why willpower and discipline, on their own, cannot override your internal patterns;
- how your thoughts, emotions, identity, and actions are either working together … or working against you;
- the invisible ways you may be reinforcing the very reality you are trying to change; and
- why consistency in who you are being matters more than intensity in what you are doing.

You are going to begin recognizing yourself more clearly. Not from a place of judgment, but from a place of awareness. Because awareness is where change actually begins. You cannot shift what you are not willing to see. And you cannot create something new while unconsciously repeating what is familiar.

This chapter is where you start to see the truth of your patterns, not to shame yourself for them, but to understand them. To meet yourself in them. And to realize that nothing about you is broken. You have simply been operating from learned responses, beliefs, and identities that once made sense, but they may no longer serve the life you are trying to create. And once you see that clearly, something powerful happens. You stop trying to force change from the outside, and you begin creating it from within.

This is the foundation for everything that follows.

Why Your Effort Isn't the Missing Piece

Most people have been taught that if they want a different life, they need to work harder.

Push more. Try longer. Fix themselves.

The message is usually some version of *grind until it happens.*

If it hasn't worked yet, you must not be doing enough.

If you're tired, you must not want it badly enough.

If you're struggling, there must be something wrong with you.

So, people double down. They wake up earlier. They push through exhaustion. They shame themselves into motivation. They turn life into a constant self-improvement project, convinced that one more effort will finally make everything click.

But effort without alignment creates burnout. Vision without embodiment creates frustration. You can't outwork an internal contradiction. And most of the time, the contradiction looks like this:

> You say you want expansion, but your body is still trained to expect danger.
>
> You say you want love, but your nervous system is still scanning for abandonment.
>
> You say you want money, but part of you believes money disappears, corrupts people, creates resentment, or requires suffering and sacrifice to earn.

So, you push harder.

You try to think more positive. You tell yourself to "stay high vibe." You repeat affirmations while your shoulders are hunched over and your breath is shallow. And then you wonder why you feel exhausted. It's because you are trying to build a new reality using an old internal operating system.

This is where most people get confused. They think they need better discipline, stronger willpower, or a more positive mindset. What they actually need is to understand what is driving their system underneath the effort.

Here's what's really running the show.

Your conscious mind may want growth, but your subconscious is designed to keep you safe. And safety, to the nervous system, means *familiar*, not necessarily happy, not even healthy, just known.

If chaos is familiar, calm can feel unsafe.

If struggle is familiar, ease can feel suspicious.

If disappointment is familiar, hope can feel dangerous.

So even as you consciously reach forward, another part of you quietly pulls the brakes. This is not self-sabotage in the way we've been taught to judge it. It's self-protection. Your energy is the missing piece.

Energy is not mystical or vague. It is the sum total of what your body believes, what your emotions practice, and what your nervous system expects. When you live in clarity, trust, gratitude, and self-belief, life meets you differently. You notice doors you used to walk past. You recover faster when things wobble. You feel supported instead of braced.

You don't have to chase alignment when you are aligned. You attract it.

When you live in fear, scarcity, resentment, or self-doubt, life feels heavier. Everything takes more effort. Delays feel personal. Momentum feels fragile. Not because you're cursed. Not because you're unlucky. Not because the universe is testing you. But because your internal state and your external desires are speaking different languages. This does not mean you are doing anything wrong. It means you are human.

Most people are not "bad at manifesting." They are simply untrained at reading and regulating their own internal state. They have never been taught how to listen to their body, work with their nervous system, or understand how belief lives beneath words. They are trying to stream a love song on a channel still set to static.

So, they blame themselves. They try harder. They get louder internally.

And the static increases.

Introducing the 24/7 Manifestation Method

You may be wondering why it's called the 24/7 Manifestation Method. And yes, part of that meaning is exactly what you think. Manifestation is not something you turn on for a few minutes a day. It is happening 24 hours a day, 7 days a week. Every thought, every reaction, every belief, every decision is shaping your reality in real time.

You are always manifesting. But the name also carries a second, more intentional layer. This method is designed to be practiced over the course of seven days. And within each of those days, you will anchor a new way of thinking and being by writing your chosen affirmation 24 times in the morning, and 24 times in the evening.

Twenty-four. Seven.

24/7.

A structure that mirrors the truth: transformation is not created in isolated moments. It is created through repetition, rhythm, and the way you show up consistently over time. The practice itself is simple. But the power comes from how it integrates into your life. Because this is not just about what you write for a few minutes in the morning and at night. It is about how you think, feel, respond, and choose throughout the rest of your day.

This is where the method becomes a lifestyle. Not something you try but something you live.

The goal of the 24/7 Manifestation Method is not to control every thought you have. That would be exhausting and unrealistic. You are not here to police your mind or suppress your emotions. The goal is to teach you how to notice your energetic state and gently guide it, on purpose, throughout your day. To recognize when you are operating from fear instead of alignment. And to give you a structure that supports that awareness, not just in theory, but in practice. While manifestation is always happening, transformation happens when you begin working with it intentionally.

The 24/7 Manifestation Method is a simple, grounded, and repeatable process designed to help you do exactly that. At its core, this is a seven-day experience. A week where you begin to interrupt old patterns, stabilize new ones, and create a different internal baseline to operate from. Each day, you will work with your mind at two of its most receptive moments, just after you wake up, and just before you fall asleep.

These are known as hypnagogic states, moments where your mind is more open, less guarded, and more impressionable. You are not fully in your analytical thinking yet, and you are not fully in rest. You are in between. And it is in this in-between space that new patterns are most easily introduced. During these windows, you will write your affirmation 24 times in the morning, and 24 times in the evening.

Not as a ritual you rush through, and not as something you perform to "get it done," but as a way of imprinting a new way of thinking, feeling, and identifying, consistently, over time. The number is not about perfection. It is about rhythm. Repetition. Reinforcement. It is about giving your mind and body enough exposure to a new narrative that it begins to feel familiar. But this method is not just about what you do for a few minutes in the morning and at night.

It is about how you live in between.

Throughout these seven days, you will also be guided through a series of practices that help you become aware of your patterns, your emotional responses, your identity, and your actions. You will begin to notice where you disconnect from the version of yourself you are calling in and you will learn how to return, in real time.

This is where the "24/7" comes to life. In your conversations, reactions, habits, decisions, and self-talk. You are not just practicing manifestation for a few minutes a day. You are learning how to embody it, consistently, gently, and in a way that actually lasts.

This is not about becoming someone new overnight. It is about creating enough aligned moments, over the course of seven days, that something begins to shift. And once it shifts, you do not go back to who you were before.

To learn how to bring your body back into safety. To shift from forcing outcomes to becoming receptive to them.

This is when manifestation stops feeling like work and starts feeling like flow.

Flow doesn't mean life becomes perfect. It means life becomes responsive.

You move, and something meets you. You choose, and clarity follows. You pause, and your body exhales.

Here is the most empowering reframe I can give you right now: If your life is not matching what you want, it is not because you are broken. It is because you are broadcasting something different than you think. And the moment you can see that, without judgment, without shame, you gain your power back. Because what can be observed can be shifted. What can be felt can be regulated. What can be understood can be rewritten.

You don't need to become someone else to create a different life. You need to come back into relationship with yourself. And that is exactly where this work begins.

The Four-part Signal: Thought, Emotion, Identity, Action

Let me make this practical. Your manifestation signal has four main channels:

Thought: what you repeatedly think, consciously and unconsciously

Emotion: what you repeatedly feel, even under the surface

Identity: who you believe you are, what you think you deserve, what feels "like you"

Action: what you do, what you avoid, what you tolerate, what you choose

When these four channels agree, you become magnetic. When they conflict, you get mixed results. You can tell yourself you are confident, but if your body feels unsafe, your identity is still "I am not safe to be seen," and your actions keep avoiding exposure, the universe reads the deeper signal.

This is why manifestation cannot be only mental. It is energetic. It is behavioral. It is embodied. It is you, as a whole being, becoming congruent with what you desire. Congruence is the secret sauce that people call luck. It is not luck. It is alignment.

MEET THE REAL DRIVER: YOUR SUBCONSCIOUS MIND

It stores your habits, beliefs, emotional patterns, and automatic reactions. It decides what feels safe, familiar, or threatening, and then steers your behavior accordingly. You have a conscious mind that makes goals. And you have a subconscious mind that keeps you alive. The subconscious is not interested in your vision board. It is interested in survival. It is interested in what is familiar. It is interested in keeping you within the boundaries of what you have known.

So, if your conscious goal is "I want more," but your subconscious belief is "More is unsafe," you are going to feel resistance. That resistance doesn't mean you're not meant for your desire. It means you are expanding beyond your current safety threshold. That's actually good news because it tells you exactly where the work is.

Research suggests the majority of your daily decisions are influenced by subconscious programming. That means your conscious goals are often negotiating with outdated internal settings you did not consciously choose.

Here is the empowering part: your brain is not fixed.

Thanks to neuroplasticity, your brain rewires itself based on repetition, emotion, and focus. The thoughts you repeat, the emotions you practice, and the identity you reinforce reshape your neural pathways over time. You are not stuck with the brain you were handed. You are not stuck with the conditioning you inherited. You are not stuck with the patterns you learned. You can rewire. But you cannot rewire with only occasional inspiration. You rewire with consistent practice.

And there are two especially powerful windows when this rewiring happens more easily: right after you wake up and right before you fall asleep. These moments, often referred to as hypnagogic or liminal states, are when your subconscious is most impressionable. Your critical mind is quieter. Your brain is more suggestible. You are more receptive to new programming.

That is why the 24/7 Manifestation Method anchors key practices in these windows. When you introduce a clear intention paired with emotion during these times, you bypass resistance and speak directly to the subconscious. Think of your subconscious as fertile soil. Thoughts are seeds. Emotion is water and sunlight. Repetition is the growing season. Identity is the garden you choose to live in. This is not fluffy. This is how humans learn. This is how habits form. Some shifts happen immediately. Others take time not because the work didn't "work," but because your subconscious was quietly rerouting you toward something you couldn't yet see. I've watched people finish this method convinced nothing changed, only to realize months later that everything had. This is how you become someone new.

Why "Positive Thinking" Isn't the Point

Let's talk about the lie that has confused an entire generation of manifestors: if you think positively enough, your life will change. Listen, positive thinking can be helpful. It can be a tool. It can be a doorway out of a spiral. But it is not the foundation because you can think positively while still feeling unsafe. You can think positively while still believing you're unworthy. You can think positively while still living in patterns that contradict what you want. The universe does not respond to the sentence you post on Instagram. It responds to the frequency you live in.

They did the affirmation. They did the vision board. They did the scripting. But their nervous system was broadcasting a completely different message. Your body was still saying, "No." Your habits were still saying, "Not me." Your identity was still saying, "That's for other people." You do not attract what you casually wish for. You attract what you are congruent with. When your inner world agrees with your desires, things begin to move with surprising ease. When it doesn't, life feels resistant, no matter how hard you try.

Fear, scarcity, frustration, and doubt feel heavy in the body. Days take more effort. Momentum feels fragile. Setbacks land harder than they should. Most people aren't bad at manifesting. They're living inside an internal climate they've never been taught how to notice. Your job isn't to control every thought. It's to become aware of the state you're living in and to guide it, gently, on purpose.

I've watched people come into this work believing they were stuck in careers, relationships, or even their own homes. One woman realized the heaviness she felt each morning wasn't coming from her schedule or her circumstances. It was coming from the energy she lived inside. When that shifted, movement returned almost immediately.

Sometimes what we call *reality* is actually just a conclusion we formed during pain and then kept repeating until it felt like fact. I've seen people swear they were unlovable, unlucky, or doomed to repeat the same relationships, only to realize those beliefs were born in a single moment of betrayal or loss, not in truth.

Let's make this painfully real.

Say you repeat, "I am confident with money." You say it out loud. You write it on a sticky note. You even say it with a cute little smile because you saw someone on TikTok say smiling helps. But your body tightens when you check your bank app. You avoid looking at bills. You tell your friend, "Money is just hard for me."

Your words say: confident.

Your nervous system says: unsafe.

Your behavior says: avoid.

That's not failure. It's information.

And awareness is where everything begins.

Your subconscious will always prioritize your felt reality over your spoken words.

Identity Is the Engine

Here is one of the most important truths: You do not manifest what you want. You manifest who you are.

Your current reality reflects your self-concept, the story you carry about who you are and what is possible for you. If you want a new life, you must first become the version of you who naturally lives it. Identity shifting is not pretending. It is preparing.

When you begin thinking, feeling, and acting like your future self before the evidence arrives, reality catches up quickly. Your brain loves consistency. It loves to confirm what you believe about yourself. So, if you believe "I am the kind of person who follows through," you will notice yourself following through more often. If you believe "I am always behind," your brain will find evidence of behindness everywhere. If you believe "I am hard to love," your nervous system will interpret neutral moments as rejection.

Identity is the filter. Identity is the engine. Identity is the script your life is reading from.

I've seen people who spent their lives people-pleasing suddenly become the person others listened to. Not because they demanded respect but because they stopped abandoning themselves.

The Body Never Lies

Your body is one of the most honest indicators of alignment. You can say affirmations all day long, but your body reveals what you truly feel safe receiving. If your jaw tightens while you say, "I am abundant," your nervous system is signaling a threat. If your chest contracts when you imagine love, your body is holding an old story.

This is not a failure. It is information. Manifestation responds to safety. When your body feels regulated and supported, your energy becomes coherent. And coherence is magnetic.

Throughout the next chapters, you will learn how to listen to your body, work with your nervous system, and gently retrain it to feel safe with expansion. Because sometimes the thing that is blocking your manifestation is not your mindset. It is your nervous system.

You cannot white-knuckle your way into receiving. You must teach your body that receiving is safe.

Let me show you what this looks like in a real body, not just in theory. I want to share a real-life story with you that illustrates this more clearly than any metaphor ever could.

Tara attended one of my retreats in Costa Rica. She was convinced she struggled with her weight, and no matter what she tried, she couldn't lose it. She talked about it casually at first, almost apologetically, the way so many women do. As if her body was an inconvenience she needed to explain. As if her size was something she owed the room an excuse for.

She had tried everything over the years. Diets that promised discipline. Programs that promised control. Meal plans, workouts, willpower, shame disguised as motivation.

She spoke about her body like it was an opponent. Something to fight. Something to override. Something to deal with. Something that had betrayed her and now needed to be conquered.

And I want to pause here, because this language is so common we barely notice it.

"I'm fighting my body."

"I hate my body."

"My body won't cooperate."

But bodies do not resist without reason.

As the week unfolded, and she began practicing the 24/7 Manifestation Method, writing in the quiet of the morning, reflecting in the safety of the container, regulating her nervous system, listening instead of forcing, something deeper started to surface. Not all at once. Slowly. Gently. Like a truth that had been waiting for permission to emerge.

One afternoon, during a journaling exercise, her hands began to shake. She stopped writing. She put the pen down. And with a slight quiver in her voice, she told us something she had never said out loud in a room full of people.

She had previously experienced 11 miscarriages.

Eleven.

Not one or two. Eleven cycles of hope and loss. Eleven times letting herself imagine a future, only to have it taken away. Eleven times her body carried life and then didn't.

And somewhere along the way, quietly, unconsciously, without drama or declaration, she made a decision: "My body failed me."

Not as a sentence she consciously thought. Not as words she would ever say out loud. But as a belief that settled into her cells. This is how beliefs are formed. Not through logic, but through experience. Through moments that overwhelm the nervous system. Through pain that has nowhere to go.

When the body becomes associated with loss, betrayal, or danger, the nervous system shifts into protection mode. It does not ask permission. It does not consult your goals. It simply does what it was designed to do. **It protects**.

And in many cases, weight is not about lack of discipline. It is not about laziness. It is not about failure. It is about safety. It is armor. It is insulation. It is the body saying, "Please don't hurt me again."

Her weight was not the problem. It was the strategy.

Once this truth surfaced, something profound happened. Not externally. Internally. For the first time in years, she stopped trying to punish her body into submission and started listening to it. She grieved. Not just the miscarriages, but the years she had spent at war with herself. The years of resentment. The years of believing she was broken.

She honored what her body had endured. She acknowledged the strength it took to survive that much loss. She let herself feel sadness instead of overriding it with control. And slowly, the belief began to loosen.

"I'm not broken," she said one night, her voice barely above a whisper. "My body didn't fail me."

When that belief dissolved, her body no longer needed protection in the same way.

A year later, she sent me a video message. She was vibrant like I had never seen before and smiling ear to ear as she shared that she had released approximately 100 pounds.

Not through force or restriction. And definitely not through hatred. But through reconciliation. More importantly, she told me something that mattered even more. She felt at peace. She was present with the living children she had. She looked in the mirror with gratitude instead of resentment or avoidance. She no longer felt like she needed to disappear to be safe.

Her body hadn't failed her.

I want you to hear this because it may be the missing key for you. Maybe your body is not resisting you. Maybe your body is responding. Maybe your anxiety is not a flaw. Maybe it is a signal.

Maybe your exhaustion is not laziness. Maybe it is grief.

Maybe the pattern you keep trying to "fix" is actually a strategy that once kept you safe. And when you listen to the message instead of fighting the symptom, the strategy can shift.

Nothing in you is broken.

There is wisdom in your patterns. There is intelligence in your coping. There is a reason behind every behavior your body learned to keep you alive.

This work is not about forcing change. It is about creating enough safety for change to happen naturally. And when safety arrives, the body releases what it no longer needs to carry.

You will drift. That does not mean you are failing. The goal is not perfection, but repair. Powerful manifestors are not the ones who never wobble. They are the ones who return to themselves quickly.

Grandma's Wisdom

I was raised by a grandmother who could heal with spices and stories. She taught me that words carry weight and choices carry light. Years later, neuroscience gave me language for what she already knew:

Your brain changes when you ask it to. Your body changes when you treat it like a friend. Your life changes when you live as if your future is already in the room.

Let's write it together, page by page, day by day. You've already begun.

As you move through this book, you'll meet people who believed they were broken, unlucky, or stuck. You'll see how grief hid behind habits, how fear dressed itself up as logic, and how identity, not effort, changed the trajectory of their lives. None of them were special. They were simply willing to listen.

You do not need to fix yourself to create a different life. You need to understand yourself. That understanding is where your power begins. And as you keep reading, I'll show you how to build it, step by step, in a way your body can actually trust.

Closing: An Invitation to Begin

If you are reading this, something in you already knows. You are ready to stop manifesting by default and start manifesting on purpose. Not someday. Not when you feel ready. Now.

You do not have to be perfect to be powerful. Power begins with intention. Intention in how you think, how you feel, and the stories you allow to shape you.

You are the creator of your own reality, and this is where the intentional shift in your life begins. Not with a wish, but with a decision. Your future isn't waiting for you. It's responding to you. And before you can consciously create something new, you must understand what you are already creating and why.

In the next chapter, we are going to look beneath the surface of your current reality. Not to judge it, but to decode it, to understand the patterns, beliefs, and internal responses that have been shaping your life up until now. Once you see clearly what is driving your results, you stop guessing and you start creating with intention.

Reflection Questions

1. Where in your life do you notice the biggest gap between what you want and how you feel?
2. What belief did you adopt during a painful moment that might still be shaping your life?
3. What would change if you began acting like the version of you who already trusts herself?

CHAPTER 2

Why Most Manifestation Methods Don't Work (And Why This One Does)

If manifestation worked the way it's often sold online, the world would look very different by now.

People would write an affirmation once. Light a candle. Visualize for a few minutes. And then wake up inside a life that finally made sense. There would be no confusion. No second-guessing. No quiet wondering if it was ever "working" in the first place.

But that's not what happens.

What actually happens is far more human.

People usually come to manifestation in moments of hope. Or exhaustion. Or longing. Something cracks open and triggers a desire for something to change. A relationship ends. A bank balance dips. A body sends a signal that can't be ignored. And in that moment, the idea that you can intentionally shape your life feels like oxygen. Like relief. Like maybe you're not as stuck as it feels.

They feel inspired, maybe even relieved. They start journaling. Visualizing. Repeating phrases that sound like possibility. For a few days, sometimes even a week, things feel lighter. More spacious. There's a sense of forward movement. A feeling of *maybe this time.*

And then life interrupts. A bill arrives that wasn't planned for. A partner disappoints them in a way that hits an old wound.

A body symptom flares. A doubt creeps in quietly, almost politely, asking, *What if this doesn't work either?*

And suddenly, the method "stops working."

Not because anything magical broke. Not because the universe changed its mind.

But because the method was never designed to meet a human being in motion.

This is the part that rarely gets talked about.

Manifestation doesn't fail because people don't want it badly enough. It fails because most methods don't account for how humans actually change. They treat manifestation like a mindset problem. They treat it like a belief problem. They treat it like a visualization problem.

As if repeating the right sentence enough times could override years of conditioning, patterned responses, emotional memory, and nervous system wiring. As if desire alone could dissolve habits that were built to protect you long before you ever learned the word manifestation.

But change doesn't happen at the level of intention alone. It happens at the level of embodiment.

People don't fail to manifest because they lack clarity or desire. Their inner systems are still running on old loops while they're trying to install a new future on top of them. The mind reaches forward while the body quietly pulls the brakes. The desire is real, but the system is unconvinced.

Manifestation doesn't break down at the level of wanting. It breaks down at the level of habit. At the level of nervous system safety. At the level of identity.

A person can want abundance deeply while their body tightens at the sight of a bank account.

They can want love while bracing for disappointment every time someone gets close.

They can want ease while their nervous system is still trained to expect pressure.

And until those deeper patterns are addressed, no amount of affirmations will override the internal loops running the show. This is why so many people quietly conclude that manifestation "works for other people, but not for me."

Not because they're broken. Not because they're doing it wrong. But because they were given tools meant for moments, not methods designed for real life.

So, let's name that gap.

Not to shame it. Not to bypass it. But to finally build something that can hold you when inspiration fades, life gets loud, and your nervous system takes the wheel.

Because manifestation isn't tested when things are easy. It's tested when you're tired. When you're triggered. When you're unsure. And that's exactly where this work begins.

In this chapter, we'll look beneath the surface of your current reality and begin to understand what has actually been creating it. We'll explore the patterns, beliefs, and internal responses that have been shaping your life, often without you even realizing it, so you can finally start changing them with intention.

The Myth of "If You Believe Enough"

One of the most damaging ideas in modern spirituality is the belief that if something isn't manifesting, you must not be believing hard enough. This turns manifestation into a performance. Instead of becoming more honest, people become more controlled.

They start policing their thoughts. Suppressing fear. Judging doubt. Watching themselves constantly, scanning for anything that might be "low vibe" or out of alignment. A difficult emotion shows up and instead of listening to it, they rush to cover it. They paste a positive phrase over something that actually needs care. What often begins as hope slowly turns into self-surveillance.

People start monitoring themselves the way they think the universe is watching them. They correct thoughts mid-sentence. They apologize internally for feeling human.

They pretend they feel confident when their body is clearly saying otherwise. And then, when reality doesn't change, the shame creeps in quietly.

I must be doing it wrong. I must not be spiritual enough. I must not believe enough.

This is how manifestation becomes exhausting. Not because the work itself is wrong, but because the pressure to "do it right" creates an internal split. One part of you is trying to ascend. Another part of you is just trying to survive. And instead of being integrated, those parts are at war.

People start to distrust their own inner experience. They treat fear as a flaw instead of a signal. They see doubt as a failure instead of a normal response to expansion. And when you're constantly performing belief, you're no longer in relationship with yourself. You're managing yourself.

You can have doubts and still manifest powerfully if your actions, habits, and identity are aligned. Doubt does not disqualify you. Fear does not cancel your desires. Uncertainty does not mean you're off track. What blocks manifestation is not doubt.

It's incoherence.

You can have perfect affirmations and manifest nothing if your nervous system is still broadcasting danger. You can say all the right words while your body is bracing, your habits are avoiding, and your identity is still organized around protection instead of expansion. Manifestation does not respond to your positivity.

It responds to your pattern.

And patterns aren't changed by force. They're changed by repetition, safety, and lived practice. They're changed by how you respond *over time*, not how perfectly you perform in one inspired moment. This is where so many people get stuck.

They're trying to believe their way into a new life, when what actually changes a life is what you practice when no one is watching: How you respond when you're tired. How you speak to yourself when something doesn't work out. What you do when fear shows up instead of how quickly you try to eliminate it.

What changes a life isn't one perfect belief. It's what you practice on your most basic Tuesday.

The Tuesday when nothing dramatic is happening.

The Tuesday when the kids are loud, the inbox is full, and your energy is low.

The Tuesday when you don't feel inspired, but you still choose to show up differently.

That's where identity is shaped. That's where alignment is built. That's where manifestation actually begins to work. Not in moments of spiritual performance, but in the quiet consistency of how you live.

Why Most Methods Work for a Moment, Then Stop

Most manifestation methods are designed for moments, not lives. They work when you're motivated. When you're inspired. When you're emotionally regulated. When nothing is actively threatening your sense of safety. They work when you've just watched a powerful video.

When you've had a good conversation. When you feel hopeful enough to believe again.

In those moments, alignment feels easy.

But real life doesn't stay calm long enough for that. Children get sick. Businesses fluctuate. Bodies age. Relationships trigger old wounds. Sleep gets disrupted. Hormones shift. Grief shows up uninvited. And suddenly, the version of you who felt clear and expansive on Sunday morning is nowhere to be found by Wednesday afternoon.

When your nervous system gets activated, your subconscious takes over. That's not a personal flaw. It's biology. The subconscious is designed to move fast, rely on pattern, and default to whatever has kept you safe before. When stress enters the system, the body does not pause to ask what you *want*. It moves toward what it *knows*.

That's when old habits run the show.

You reach for distraction instead of presence. You default to people-pleasing instead of truth.

You overwork, overthink, or shut down. You abandon the practice you promised yourself you'd stick with. And then comes the quiet conclusion: *I guess it didn't work*.

This is not where manifestation fails. This is where it's actually being tested.

Most methods fail not because they're wrong, but because they stop short. They teach you what to do when you feel good, but they don't train who you are when you don't. They offer inspiration without integration. Vision without containment. Belief without nervous system support.

But motivation is unreliable. Motivation fades when you're tired, when you're overwhelmed, when life asks more of you than you planned for. And life always will.

Manifestation isn't tested when things are easy. It's tested when you're triggered, when you're unsure, when you're disappointed, when your body is in protection mode and your mind is looking for certainty. That's when alignment actually matters.

Because if a method only works when you feel good, it's not a method.

It's a mood.

A real method must work when you don't feel inspired, when your energy is low, when doubt is loud, when your system wants to revert to what's familiar. It must meet you inside your humanity, not require you to transcend it.

This is where the 24/7 Manifestation Method is fundamentally different.

It doesn't ask you to be calm all the time. It doesn't require you to stay positive. It doesn't depend on you being in a "high vibration" state to function. It trains you to stay connected to yourself under pressure. To notice when you've been pulled out of alignment and know how to return without shame. To build practices that hold you steady when life shakes. To develop an identity that doesn't collapse the moment things get uncomfortable.

Because manifestation isn't about maintaining a perfect state. It's about learning how to come back. Again and again and again. And that creates change that lasts.

The Habit Loop That Shapes Your Reality

Let's talk science for a moment, not in a cold or clinical way, but in a way that gives you leverage. The kind of science that doesn't pathologize you but actually explains things.

Behavioral neuroscience describes something called the habit loop, which governs the majority of human behavior. It doesn't govern just your obvious habits, like what you eat or how often you exercise, but your emotional habits, your relational habits, your coping habits, and the way you respond to stress when no one is watching.

Every habit follows the same basic structure:

- **Trigger**—something internal or external that cues the behavior
- **Routine**—the behavior itself
- **Reward**—the emotional payoff that reinforces it

Over time, this loop becomes automatic. And automatic is what your subconscious trusts. Your brain is constantly looking for efficiency. It wants to conserve energy. So once a loop proves itself useful, especially in moments of stress or uncertainty, the brain locks it in. It stops asking whether the habit is helpful now. It only remembers that it worked once.

This is why your entire life runs on loops like these.

You feel overwhelmed → you scroll → you dissociate

You feel insecure → you overexplain → you seek reassurance

You feel anxious → you plan obsessively → you feel momentarily safe

None of these behaviors are random. None of them mean you're weak, lazy, or self-sabotaging. They are learned responses that once served you. At some point in your life, scrolling helped you regulate. Overexplaining helped you feel accepted. Planning helped you feel in control. The reward wasn't the behavior itself. The reward was the relief. And your nervous system remembers relief. The problem isn't that these loops exist. The problem is that they keep running long after they stop serving the life you want to live.

This is where manifestation often breaks down because you cannot affirm your way out of a loop you keep rehearsing. You can say "I am calm" all day long, but if your body is still using anxiety as a strategy to feel safe, the loop will win. You can visualize abundance, but if your routine is still avoidance, overworking, or bracing for loss, the subconscious will default to what it trusts.

Reality follows repetition, not intention alone. This is why insight alone doesn't change lives. Awareness is powerful, but awareness without interruption just creates more self-judgment. Real change happens when you intervene at the level where the brain actually operates.

To change your reality, you must change the loop.

That means learning how to work with

the **trigger** instead of ignoring it,

the **routine** instead of shaming it, and

the **reward** instead of pretending you don't need it.

Maybe the trigger stays the same, but the routine shifts. Maybe the routine stays similar, but the reward becomes healthier. Maybe you learn how to meet the trigger before it hijacks the system.

This is where structure matters because structure gives your nervous system something new to rely on. It replaces chaotic coping with intentional repetition. It creates predictability where there was once panic. And when the brain feels safe enough, it becomes flexible enough to change.

Inspiration fades. Insight comes and goes. But structure stays. And when you change the loops you live inside, you don't just change what you do. You change who you are being. That's how reality actually starts to reorganize.

Why Motivation Always Loses

Motivation is emotional energy. And emotional energy fluctuates. It spikes when something feels new, hopeful, or exciting. It surges when you have a breakthrough conversation, read the right sentence at the right time, or finally feel seen by an idea. Motivation feels powerful because it gives you momentum. For a moment, everything seems possible. But motivation disappears the moment something feels uncomfortable: The moment you're tired. The moment doubt creeps in. The moment life asks for consistency instead of inspiration.

This is why people start strong and fade. Why they commit big and follow through small. Why they feel inspired on Sunday and defeated by Wednesday.

It's not because they lack discipline. It's not because they don't want it badly enough. It's because motivation was never designed to carry you through change. Motivation is reactive. It responds to feeling good. And real transformation doesn't happen in feel-good moments. It happens in repetition. In boredom. In the quiet decision to keep showing up when there's no emotional reward yet. This is where people tend to get stuck. They wait to *feel* motivated before they act. But motivation is the result of movement, not the cause of it. If you wait for motivation to return, you end up stuck in a cycle of starting over.

The 24/7 Manifestation Method is not built on motivation. It's built on design.

Design is what removes decision fatigue. It's what gives your nervous system something stable to lean on. When the structure is clear, you don't have to negotiate with yourself every day. You don't have to ask, *Do I feel like doing this?* You already know what comes next.

Design creates safety. Safety allows repetition. Repetition rewires identity. Identity shapes behavior. Behavior shapes reality. That's not philosophy. That's how humans change.

When the practice is simple, predictable, and contained, the nervous system relaxes. When the nervous system relaxes, resistance decreases. And when resistance decreases, repetition becomes possible.

You stop relying on willpower. You stop starting over. You stop making your future dependent on your mood.

And that's when manifestation becomes sustainable. Not because you're more motivated but because you've built something that works even when you're not.

Your Subconscious Doesn't Care About Your Vision Board

Your subconscious mind has one primary job: keep you alive. Not fulfilled. Not successful. Not spiritually expanded.

Alive. Simply Alive.

It does not care about your goals. It does not care about your dreams. It does not care about your potential. It does not evaluate whether your desires are reasonable or aligned with your higher calling. It is not impressed by affirmations or inspired by vision boards.

What it cares about is safety, specifically, what has felt familiar enough to keep you alive. The subconscious learns through repetition and emotional association. It catalogs experiences and quietly decides, *This kept us alive. That didn't.* Over time, those decisions harden into automatic responses. Not because they are accurate, but because they are predictable. This is why people stay in jobs they resent, relationships that drain them, or identities that no longer fit.

Not because they enjoy suffering, but because suffering is known. And known feels safer than unknown to a nervous system that learned stability through familiarity.

Change, even positive change, is inherently destabilizing. Expansion means uncertainty. Visibility means exposure. Love means vulnerability. Abundance means responsibility. To a subconscious mind trained on survival, these aren't upgrades. They're risks. So, when you decide to manifest more visibility, more love, more money, more freedom, your conscious mind may feel excited, but your subconscious often hears it as a threat.

And it responds accordingly. Not with drama, but with strategy. Procrastination appears, urging you to wait. Self-doubt speaks up, questioning your readiness. Exhaustion settles in, slowing your momentum. Distraction multiplies, pulling your attention elsewhere. And suddenly, a very reasonable-sounding explanation emerges for why now isn't the right time.

This isn't sabotage. It's protection. Your system is not trying to ruin your future. It's trying to preserve your past. It's doing exactly what it was designed to do, maintain homeostasis, keep things familiar, and avoid perceived danger.

Most manifestation methods frame these responses as resistance to overcome or mindset flaws to fix. They encourage you to push harder, think more positively, or ignore the signals altogether. But when you fight your nervous system, you create more tension. And tension never leads to sustainable change. Manifestation fails not because the subconscious is broken, but because it's misunderstood. The key is not to overpower your subconscious, but to work with it: To create conditions where expansion feels safe. To introduce change in a way that doesn't trigger alarm. To build familiarity with your future self slowly enough that your nervous system doesn't reject it.

When the body feels safe, the mind follows. When the subconscious feels included, resistance softens. And when protection relaxes, forward movement becomes possible. This is the shift the 24/7 Manifestation Method makes. It stops asking your subconscious to leap into the unknown.

And instead teaches it, gently and repeatedly, that the future you desire is not a threat. It's a new form of safety.

Why the 24/7 Manifestation Method Uses Morning and Night

The 24/7 Manifestation Method is built around biology, not wishful thinking. It works with how the human mind actually learns and changes rather than asking you to override yourself with effort. There are two moments each day when your subconscious is naturally more open:

Right after waking.

Right before sleep.

These moments are not accidental. They are transitional states, when the mind is moving between worlds of awareness. You are no longer fully asleep but not yet anchored in the noise of the day. Or you are no longer actively thinking but not yet unconscious. In both states, the usual mental guardrails soften.

Brain waves slow. The analytical, critical mind loosens its grip. Emotional material integrates more easily. This is why these windows are used in hypnosis, trauma healing, memory reconsolidation, and habit formation. Not because they're mystical, but because they're effective. The brain is more receptive. Less defensive. More plastic.

During most of the day, your mind is filtering information aggressively. It evaluates. It resists. It argues. It cross-references past experiences and looks for reasons to maintain the familiar.

Morning and night are different. In these moments, the subconscious is already keenly listening. That's why the 24/7 Manifestation Method doesn't ask you to "convince" yourself of anything. Convincing requires effort. Effort triggers resistance. Resistance reinforces old patterns. Instead, the method introduces repetition at the precise times when resistance is lowest. When you write your intention in the morning, 24 times, you're setting the tone before the day tells you who to be. Before emails, responsibilities, and expectations shape your nervous system. You're gently reminding your system of the identity you're stepping into.

When you write again at night, 24 times, you're not trying to fix the day. You're allowing the subconscious to integrate a new story while the brain is already organizing memory, emotion, and meaning. This is when learning consolidates. This is when patterns are reinforced. Over time, repetition in these windows does something subtle but powerful. The new story begins to feel familiar. And familiarity is what the subconscious trusts.

When something feels familiar, it no longer registers as a threat. When it no longer feels like a threat, the body relaxes. When the body relaxes, behavior changes without force. This is why resistance drops. Not because you overpowered it. Not because you believed harder. But because the nervous system stopped needing to protect you from the future you were introducing.

The 24/7 Manifestation Method doesn't rush this process. It doesn't demand instant belief or dramatic emotional shifts. It respects the pace at which safety is built. Morning and night become anchors. Predictable. Contained. Gentle. A rhythm your system can rely on.

And when change arrives through rhythm instead of pressure, it lasts. That's the difference between a method that inspires you for a moment and one that quietly reshapes how you live.

Why Seven Days Is the Sweet Spot

Seven days is not arbitrary. It's strategic. Change becomes possible when it feels survivable. And most people don't resist transformation because they don't want it; they resist it because it feels too big, too permanent, or too overwhelming to the nervous system.

Seven days creates a container the body can agree to. It's long enough to interrupt an old pattern. Long enough to notice what normally runs on autopilot. Long enough for repetition to begin doing its quiet work beneath the surface. And it's short enough to feel safe.

You are not asking your nervous system to reinvent your entire life. You are not demanding lifelong commitment, unwavering belief, or immediate proof. You're simply asking it to try something new for one week. That matters more than it sounds.

When the brain perceives an experience as temporary, defenses lower. Resistance softens. Curiosity replaces avoidance. The system stays open instead of bracing for impact. Seven days is also contained enough to reduce overwhelm. Overwhelm shuts down learning. It triggers survival responses. It makes even supportive practices feel like pressure. A defined beginning and end create psychological safety. The system knows when to start. It knows when it will pause. That predictability builds trust. And trust is what allows repetition.

As repetition settles in, something subtle begins to happen. The practice stops feeling like effort. It becomes familiar. Not comfortable yet but known. And known is the gateway to change. Momentum builds quietly during this phase. Not through dramatic breakthroughs, but through consistency. Through small shifts in how you respond, how you speak to yourself, how your body reacts.

Momentum is where identity starts to loosen.

You notice:

I'm showing up differently.

This doesn't feel as foreign as it did.

I'm not fighting myself as much.

That's the moment transformation takes root. Seven days is enough to prove something important to your nervous system: Change does not equal danger. Growth does not require force. And becoming someone new doesn't mean losing yourself.

It means practicing something different, long enough for your system to recognize that it's safe.

When Anxiety Stopped Running the Show

A client of mine named Hazel, described herself as "high-functioning anxious."

On the outside, her life looked good. She was capable, accomplished, and reliable. People came to her for answers. She kept things moving. She handled responsibilities. From the outside, you might even have called her successful.

On the inside, it was another story. Within her, she was constantly bracing.

Her nervous system lived in a low-grade state of urgency, even on good days. Her mind was always scanning ahead, looking for what might go wrong. She replayed conversations long after they ended. She overthought decisions that didn't actually need that much weight. Even moments that were meant to feel relaxing carried an undercurrent of tension.

She told me, very matter-of-factly, "This is just how I am."

That sentence matters more than most people realize. When a pattern becomes identity, it stops being questioned. Anxiety wasn't something she experienced. It was something she believed she *was*. When she started the 24/7 Manifestation Method, she wasn't asking for something flashy. She wasn't trying to manifest more money, a new relationship, or a big external shift. She simply wanted peace. Not the Instagram version of peace. Real peace. The kind where her body could exhale. The kind she could relax into.

As she followed the daily structure, something unexpected happened. Nothing dramatic. No emotional explosions. No sudden epiphanies.

She started noticing her body felt different.

For the first time, she paid attention to the physical sensations that accompanied her thoughts and decisions. She noticed that every time she made a choice, even a small one, her chest tightened. When she tried to rest, guilt surged through her system like an alarm. When she imagined ease, her stomach flipped, as if calm itself were suspicious.

This wasn't a mindset issue. She already *knew* she didn't need to be this tense. She had read the books. Tried the affirmations. Understood the logic.

This was a nervous system pattern.

Her body had learned that staying alert meant staying safe. Urgency had become familiar. Stillness felt foreign. To the nervous system, unfamiliar often registers as a threat. Instead of forcing calm or trying to "think positive," she practiced regulation. Small, intentional moments of pause. Breathing when triggered instead of pushing through. Letting an emotion move through her body instead of immediately analyzing it. She didn't try to eliminate anxiety. She learned how to stop obeying it.

When her system activated, she didn't panic about the activation. She noticed it. She stayed with herself. She gave her body evidence, again and again, that nothing bad happened when she slowed down. Within days, subtle shifts began to occur. Her decision-making changed. She stopped catastrophizing minor choices. She stopped outsourcing reassurance to other people. She noticed that her first instinct, the one she usually second-guessed, was often clear and grounded.

She began trusting herself not because she felt suddenly confident, but because her body felt safer. Nothing dramatic happened externally that week. Her circumstances didn't radically change. Her to-do list didn't disappear. Life stayed life.

But internally, everything reorganized.

A month later, she told me something that stopped me in my tracks: "I don't feel like I'm fighting myself anymore."

That's alignment.

Not the absence of challenge, not constant calm, but the end of the internal war. The moment when your energy stops being consumed by self-monitoring, self-correcting, and self-protecting. And that's what allows manifestation to land. Because when your nervous system is no longer braced against life, your energy becomes coherent. Your choices become clearer. Your actions stop contradicting your desires.

You don't have to force outcomes when you're no longer fighting yourself. That's the power of emotional alignment. And that's what this work is really about.

Manifestation Is Not Passive

Let's clear this up because confusion here causes a lot of unnecessary frustration: manifestation is not the practice of doing nothing. And it is also not doing everything. It's not sitting back and waiting for the universe to rescue you. And it's not grinding yourself into exhaustion trying to make something happen. Both extremes miss the point.

Manifestation is about movement, but it's a very specific kind of movement. It's doing the right things from the right internal state. Action taken from fear creates more fear. It tightens the system.

It rushes the process. It reinforces the belief that if you stop pushing, everything will fall apart. That kind of action might produce short-term results, but it rarely produces peace, sustainability, or alignment. Action taken from alignment feels different. It's quieter, clearer, more efficient. It doesn't require convincing or forcing. It comes from a place of internal permission rather than pressure.

The 24/7 Manifestation Method doesn't remove action from the equation. It refines the source of action. Instead of asking, *What should I do to make this happen?* you begin asking, *What feels true to take from here?* Instead of reacting to urgency, you respond to clarity. You still send the email. You still have the conversation. You still take the step. But you do it without the internal collapse, without abandoning yourself, without overriding your body's signals.

When action comes from alignment, it builds momentum instead of burnout. It creates openings instead of resistance. And over time, it teaches your nervous system that forward movement can feel safe. That's when manifestation stops feeling like work and starts feeling like cooperation.

Why Repetition Feels Boring and Why It Works

The conscious mind loves novelty. It gets excited by new ideas, fresh rituals, and dramatic insights. The subconscious, however, loves repetition. It trusts what is familiar, predictable, and practiced. This difference is one of the biggest reasons people quit just before things begin to change. When you start a new practice, the conscious mind is engaged. It feels hopeful. Curious. Motivated. But as repetition sets in, the novelty fades. The practice starts to feel ordinary. Mechanical. Even boring. And boredom often gets misinterpreted as a sign that nothing is happening.

In reality, boredom is often a sign that something *is* happening beneath the surface. Around the same point for many people, a few days in, sometimes toward the end of the week, resistance begins to show up. Doubt whispers. The mind starts negotiating. *Do I really need to keep doing this? Shouldn't I feel different by now?* That inner friction doesn't mean the method isn't working. It usually means the old identity is being challenged.

Repetition threatens the familiar story of who you've been. It disrupts automatic patterns. It asks the nervous system to tolerate something new long enough for it to feel safe. That's uncomfortable. And discomfort often disguises itself as boredom or impatience. Resistance is not a red light. It's a threshold.

It's the moment when your system is deciding whether this new way of being is temporary or trustworthy. If you stop at the first wave of resistance, the old pattern wins by default. If you stay, gently and consistently, the new pattern begins to settle. Repetition is how safety is built. Safety is how identity shifts. And identity is what ultimately changes your life.

This is why the most powerful work often looks simple on the outside and profound on the inside.

When Nothing Changes ... Until Everything Does

One of the biggest misunderstandings about manifestation is timing. Many people expect external change to show up immediately, as proof that the work is "working." They look for signs in the outer world first, a message, an opportunity, a result, and when those don't appear right away, they assume nothing is happening.

But most transformation happens internally before it ever becomes visible. Beliefs begin to soften. The rigid stories you've been telling yourself lose their grip. Perception widens just enough for you to see options that were always there but previously felt unavailable. Your reactions shift. Your tolerance for certain patterns decreases. Your sense of what is possible expands quietly, without fireworks.

These changes are subtle, which is why they're often dismissed. They don't feel dramatic. They don't announce themselves. But they are the foundation for everything that comes next. By the time an external shift finally arrives, the opportunity, the conversation, the decision, the breakthrough, it often feels almost inevitable. Not because you forced it, and not because something suddenly changed overnight, but because your internal world has been preparing for it all along.

This is not magic. It's alignment catching up to reality. The outer world moves when the inner world is ready to receive. And readiness is rarely loud. It's steady. It's grounded. It's the quiet moment when effort drops and clarity takes its place. If you're in a phase where it feels like nothing is happening, trust that something is reorganizing. The absence of visible movement does not mean absence of progress. Often, it means the deepest work is underway.

Why This Method Works When Others Don't

This method works because it doesn't ask you to bypass fear or pretend it isn't there. It teaches you how to regulate it.

Fear is not treated as an enemy to defeat but as information to work with.

When fear is met with safety instead of resistance, it stops running the system from the background. It works because it doesn't shame doubt. Doubt is not framed as a personal failure or a sign you're "out of alignment." Instead, the method builds stability underneath doubt so that it doesn't derail you. When the body feels supported, uncertainty no longer has the power to collapse momentum.

This method also doesn't rely on belief alone. Belief is unreliable when it's not backed by behavior. You can believe something intellectually and still live in patterns that contradict it. This approach addresses that gap by working with habits, nervous system responses, and identity, the places where change actually takes hold. It works because it rewires habit rather than chasing inspiration. It recognizes that transformation happens through repetition, not intensity. Through structure that feels supportive instead of rigid, new patterns become familiar, and familiar is what the subconscious trusts.

Finally, this method works because it doesn't promise instant gratification. It delivers sustainable change. Instead of creating temporary highs followed by collapse, it builds a foundation that can hold expansion over time. You don't just experience change; you become someone who can live inside it. That's the difference.

Closing: What Comes Next

In the next chapter, we'll go deeper into the science *and* the spirit of manifestation, not as separate ideas, but as parts of the same system. You'll begin to see how your brain, your body, and your energy field are constantly in conversation with one another, shaping the reality you experience moment to moment. Not symbolically. Literally.

We'll explore how your nervous system influences your decisions before you're aware of them. How repetition reshapes neural pathways. How emotional states become default patterns. And how identity, once formed, quietly organizes your choices, reactions, and opportunities. This isn't about piling on more concepts. It's about understanding the mechanics so that you can stop blaming yourself for patterns you were never taught how to change.

For now, let this settle.

Manifestation doesn't fail because you're doing it wrong. It fails because most methods never taught you how to live differently inside your actual life with its interruptions, emotions, history, and responsibilities. They taught you what to think, but not how to respond. What to visualize, but not how to regulate. What to want, but not how to become.

That's what we're doing here. We're not chasing peak moments or perfect beliefs. We're building something that works on ordinary days, under pressure, and in real bodies. Something that can hold expansion without collapse.

Change doesn't happen all at once. It happens in loops, in small, repeated choices, in how you meet yourself when things wobble, and in who you practice being when no one is watching.

One loop at a time. One day at a time. One identity shift at a time.

That's how a different life is built.

Reflection Questions

1. Where have you relied on motivation instead of structure?
2. Which habit loops do you recognize in your own life?
3. Where might resistance be a sign of identity shift, not failure?
4. What would change if you committed to seven days without judging the outcome?

You don't need to believe perfectly. You need to practice consistently.

CHAPTER 3

The Science and Spirit of Becoming: How Your Brain, Body, and Energy Field Create Your Reality

At some point in your life, you were taught that change happens through force.

Work harder.

Try again.

Push through.

Override your feelings.

Stay disciplined.

Don't slow down.

That model works for machines. It works for systems built to perform on command.

It does not work for humans. Humans are not wired to transform through pressure. We are wired to change through repetition, safety, and meaning. We change through experiences that teach the body something new, not through thoughts that demand compliance, through environments that feel supportive enough for growth, not through shame disguised as motivation.

Most people don't fail to change because they lack willpower. They fail because they are trying to evolve inside systems that still feel unsafe. They are asking their nervous system to expand while it is braced for survival. They are asking their body to trust a future that has not yet been proven safe to receive. This is where so much spiritual teaching and so much personal development go wrong. It asks you to override your humanity instead of working with it.

This chapter is where spirituality and neuroscience stop arguing and start collaborating. This is where ancient wisdom and modern science arrive at the same truth from different directions: your reality changes when your internal systems learn something new. Not when you want harder. Not when you visualize longer. Not when you shame yourself into becoming "better."

Change happens when your brain forms new pathways through repetition.

When your nervous system learns that something unfamiliar is not a threat.

When your body stops bracing and starts participating.

When your energy field becomes coherent instead of fragmented.

This is not about fixing yourself. It's about updating what your system believes is possible, safe, and available. It's about learning how to become someone new without abandoning who you are.

Becoming is not an act of force. It's a process of alignment.

When your brain rewires, your nervous system recalibrates, and your energy field coheres, reality reorganizes naturally around you. It's not because you tried harder, but because you changed at the level where change actually lasts.

That is becoming.

In this chapter, we'll talk about what it actually means to become the version of yourself who already has what you desire. Not as an idea you visit when you feel motivated, but as an identity you begin to embody consistently. We'll explore how your brain forms and reinforces patterns, how your nervous system determines what feels safe or unsafe for you to receive, and how your sense of self quietly dictates the results you allow into your life.

You'll begin to see that manifestation is not about getting something outside of you. It is about becoming someone different within you. And once that shift begins, your thoughts change. Your choices change. Your standards change. And eventually your reality follows.

Why Becoming Comes Before Having

Most people try to manifest from the outside in. They believe the change must arrive first.

"If I get the thing, I'll feel safe."

"If I meet the person, I'll feel worthy."

"If I make the money, I'll finally relax."

This logic feels reasonable. It's how we're taught to think about cause and effect. But the body doesn't work that way. The nervous system doesn't wait for proof and then respond. It responds first, and reality organizes around that response.

Safety comes first. Then expansion. Then results.

If the body does not feel safe, it will not sustain change, no matter how badly the mind wants it. You can intellectually desire something while your nervous system quietly resists it. And when that happens, the body always wins.

This is why the phrase "act as if" so often backfires. Without nervous system support, acting as if feels like pretending. It feels like performance. It feels like pressure. You're asking your system to behave as though something is true before it has learned that it's safe. That creates exhaustion instead of alignment. The issue isn't that people aren't trying hard enough. It's that they're trying to leap ahead of their own capacity.

The 24/7 Manifestation Method is not about pretending to be someone you're not. It doesn't ask you to override your instincts or silence your body. It asks you to train your system gently and consistently, so that a future version of you no longer feels unfamiliar or threatening.

When safety is established, something remarkable happens. The brain becomes more flexible. The body relaxes its grip. Behavior shifts without force. You stop pushing yourself into change and start moving toward it naturally. Once the system feels safe, expansion doesn't require effort. It becomes the next logical step.

And when expansion is embodied, results follow as a consequence, not a chase.

Neuroplasticity: Your Brain Is Not Fixed

For a long time, science believed the brain stopped changing after childhood. The idea was that personality, habits, and capacity were largely fixed by early life and that adulthood was mostly about managing what you were given.

We now know that is false.

Your brain is plastic. That means it remains capable of change throughout your entire life. It rewires itself constantly in response to experience. Not dramatic experiences only, but ordinary ones. The way you think, the emotions you return to, the behaviors you repeat, and the environments you move through all shape your neural architecture over time.

This ongoing ability to change is called neuroplasticity.

Every thought you think strengthens a neural pathway. Not because the thought is true, but because it is familiar. Every emotion you rehearse reinforces a pattern in the nervous system. And every behavior you repeat becomes more efficient, more automatic, and easier to default to the next time stress appears. Your brain does not judge what you practice. It records it.

This is why insight alone doesn't create change. You can understand something intellectually and still live inside the same patterns. The brain learns through repetition and emotional relevance, not intention. You are always wiring something, whether you're aware of it or not. You're either reinforcing old circuits or building new ones. There is no neutral state.

So, the question is not whether you are changing.

The question is what you are changing *toward.*

Are you wiring your future, or are you unconsciously rehearsing your past?

The Brain Learns Through Experience, Not Logic

Here's an important distinction: Your conscious mind learns through information.

Your subconscious learns through experience.

You can read a book, hear a truth, nod along, and genuinely agree with it intellectually. You can understand that you are worthy, capable, and deserving of more. And yet, when you're faced with an opportunity, a relationship, or a moment of visibility, your body might still tighten. You might hesitate. You might pull back. That disconnect isn't a failure of belief. It's a mismatch between knowledge and embodiment.

Understanding does not equal embodiment.

The subconscious doesn't update because something makes sense. It updates when it *feels lived.* When a new experience is repeated often enough, with enough emotional relevance, the body begins to recognize it as familiar. And familiar is what the nervous system trusts.

Embodiment happens when four things begin to line up, not once, but repeatedly:

Your thoughts

Your emotions

Your physical sensations

Your behavior

When you think differently but still act the same, the brain doesn't change.

When you act differently but feel unsafe doing it, the brain resists.

But when thought, emotion, sensation, and behavior start telling the same story, even in small ways, a signal is sent inward.

That signal says: "This is who we are now."

And the brain listens. Once the brain accepts a new identity as real, it reorganizes automatically. Neural pathways shift. Habits soften. Responses become more fluid. You stop forcing change and start living inside it. This is why sustainable transformation doesn't come from convincing yourself. It comes from giving your system repeated evidence that a new way of being is safe, possible, and real.

That is embodiment.

The Nervous System Is the Gatekeeper

Your nervous system is constantly deciding what feels safe, threatening, or overwhelming. It does this quietly, beneath conscious thought, scanning your internal state and your environment for cues. Long before the mind weighs in, the body has already made an assessment.

This system evolved to keep you alive, not to help you achieve your goals. It tracks tone of voice, facial expression, pace, uncertainty, and emotional charge. It remembers what led to safety and what led to pain, and it responds accordingly. This is why reactions often feel automatic—because they are.

When your nervous system feels safe, your entire internal world changes. Creativity expands because the brain has the capacity to explore. Clarity sharpens because energy isn't being spent on protection. Intuition becomes accessible because the body isn't bracing. Energy flows because the system isn't contracted.

When the nervous system feels unsafe, the opposite happens. Focus narrows to immediate threat. Fear becomes louder than reason. Old habits take over because they are familiar and efficient. Contraction rules, not because something is wrong, but because the body believes it needs to protect you.

Manifestation does not override this system. It cannot be forced through willpower or positive thinking. It works with the nervous system, not against it. This is why someone can intellectually want more love, visibility, success, expansion, and yet physically freeze when opportunity appears. The desire is real, but the body doesn't experience the moment as safe.

The body doesn't respond to desire.

It responds to safety.

When safety is present, movement becomes natural. When it isn't, resistance is not a flaw. It's information.

Why Regulation Is Power, Not Weakness

Many people associate emotional regulation with suppression. They imagine it means swallowing feelings, numbing discomfort, or forcing themselves into a state of artificial calm. They think regulation looks like being unbothered, unreactive, and composed at all times.

That's not regulation. That's disconnection. True regulation doesn't eliminate emotion. It allows emotion to move. It means staying present with sensation instead of fleeing it. It means letting the body complete a stress response rather than trapping it through overthinking, distraction, or self-judgment. Regulation is not about never getting activated. It's about how quickly and gently you return to baseline once you do.

When an emotion arises and is met with awareness instead of resistance, the nervous system receives an important message: This is tolerable. This is survivable. We don't need to escalate. Over time, that message rewires how the system responds to stress. Emotions stop feeling dangerous. Activation stops turning into overwhelm. The body learns that it can feel deeply without losing control.

A regulated nervous system still feels fear, sadness, anger, and excitement. The difference is that those emotions move through instead of taking over. They inform rather than hijack. They become signals instead of commands.

This matters for manifestation because expansion brings sensation. Growth brings uncertainty. New levels of visibility, intimacy, or responsibility naturally activate the nervous system. If your system cannot process emotion, it will shut down expansion to protect you.

But when your system can process emotion, it can hold more. More opportunities. More ease. More aliveness. Regulation isn't about staying calm. It's about staying present. And presence is what allows growth to land without collapse.

Real-world Case Study: When Overthinking Was a Survival Skill

I worked with a woman named Pamela who believed she was "bad at trusting herself." That was the story she told about herself, calmly and convincingly, as if it were a personality trait rather than a pattern.

Pamela overthought everything. She second-guessed even simple decisions. She replayed conversations in her head long after they were over, analyzing tone, timing, and meaning. She could see 10 steps ahead, anticipate reactions, and imagine every possible outcome. From the outside, it looked like intelligence. Inside, it felt exhausting.

She assumed the problem was confidence.

If she could just believe in herself more, everything would settle.

But confidence was never the issue.

As we explored her patterns, it became clear that overthinking had once been a survival skill. In earlier environments, being able to read the room, predict emotional shifts, and stay mentally alert had kept her safe. Thinking ahead meant avoiding conflict. Preparation meant protection. Her nervous system had learned a simple rule:

"If I think far enough ahead, I survive."

The problem wasn't overthinking.

The problem was that the pattern never updated.

Through the 24/7 Manifestation Method, Pamela didn't try to stop overthinking or force herself into trust. She focused on something much more foundational: safety. She began teaching her body that the present moment wasn't dangerous. She practiced breathing through decisions instead of rushing to resolve them. She paused before reacting instead of immediately explaining herself. She allowed emotions to move through her body without dissecting them for meaning. Nothing dramatic. Nothing performative. Just repeated moments of staying with herself.

As safety increased, the overthinking softened on its own. Her intuition, which had always been there beneath the noise, became clearer. Decisions took less effort. Her energy stabilized. She felt less scattered and more anchored.

Manifestation followed.

Not because she changed her thoughts.

But because her nervous system learned it was safe to let go.

That's what real change looks like.

The Body as an Information System

Your body is not separate from manifestation. It is central to it.

The body is where experience is stored. Not as stories or thoughts, but as sensation, reflex, and pattern. It holds emotional memory, learned beliefs, trauma responses, and deeply ingrained safety strategies. Long before the mind forms a narrative, the body has already decided what feels safe, what feels risky, and what requires protection.

This is why manifestation cannot live only in the mind. You can say an affirmation and feel soothed one day, grounded in possibility, open to receiving. And the very next day, that same sentence can trigger tightness, resistance, or irritation. The words didn't change. Your body did. Or more accurately, your body is responding to what else is happening in your life, your stress levels, your sense of stability, and your current capacity.

The body is constantly checking in:

Is this true yet?

Is this familiar?

Is this safe to believe?

Is it safe to receive?

When the answer is no, the system applies the brakes. Not as punishment, but as protection. Manifestation stalls not because you're doing something wrong but because the body is unconvinced. When the answer becomes yes, even subtly, things begin to move with surprising ease. Decisions feel clearer. Actions feel more natural. Opportunities are recognized instead of avoided.

This is why embodiment matters. Manifestation doesn't respond to what you say you want. It responds to what your body is ready to allow.

Coherence: When Everything Starts Speaking the Same Language

Coherence is the state where your thoughts, emotions, body, and actions are aligned. Nothing is fighting anything else inside you. There is no inner tug-of-war, no part of you saying yes while another quietly says no.

In neuroscience, coherence refers to organized, efficient brain activity. Signals travel smoothly. Less energy is wasted on internal conflict. In physics, coherence describes waves moving in harmony, reinforcing one another instead of canceling each other out. The same principle applies to your inner world.

In lived experience, coherence feels like clarity without urgency. Flow without forcing. Grounded confidence that doesn't need to prove itself. Ease that still contains movement and responsibility. This is the state where manifestation accelerates, not because you're doing more, but because nothing inside you is pulling in the opposite direction. When your system speaks one clear language, reality responds more quickly.

Timelines and the Quantum Field (Without Losing Your Mind)

When people hear phrases like *quantum field* or *multiple timelines*, the mind often jumps to something abstract or untethered from daily life. But at its most grounded level, this idea is simple: at any given moment, there are many possible versions of how your life could unfold. Not mystical versions, but practical ones. Different outcomes based on different choices, different reactions, different ways of responding to the same circumstances. You already know this intuitively. You've lived moments where one decision changed everything. That's not magic. That's potential organizing into reality.

Think of these possibilities as existing in a field of options. Not all at once in a dramatic sense, but as available paths. The version you step into is not selected by wishing or hoping. It's selected by what you consistently reinforce. Your identity, your attention, and your behavior act like a tuning mechanism. They narrow the field. They determine which options become accessible and which quietly fall away.

This is where coherence matters. When your thoughts point in one direction, your body braces in another, and your habits pull you backward, the signal you send is fragmented. Fragmented signals don't collapse into clear outcomes. But when your internal systems begin to agree, when what you think, feel, and do start moving together, the signal strengthens. That coherence makes certain timelines more likely, not because the universe rewards you, but because your system is finally aligned enough to sustain them.

You don't wish yourself into a new timeline. You habituate into it through repeated choices, familiar emotional states, and actions that match who you are becoming. Over time, the version of you that once felt like a stretch starts to feel normal. And when something feels normal, the brain stops resisting it. That's how possibility turns into lived reality.

Why the Energy Field Is Not "Woo"

Your body generates an electromagnetic field. This is not metaphorical. It is measurable and observable. Every electrical impulse in your nervous system, every rhythmic beat of your heart, contributes to a field of information that extends beyond your physical body. In particular, the heart produces one of the strongest electromagnetic fields in the body, radiating outward and interacting with the environment around you.

This field is not static. It changes based on your internal state. When you are emotionally coherent, when your thoughts, emotions, and physiology are working together, the field becomes more ordered and stable. When you are stressed, fragmented, or dysregulated, the field becomes erratic. The signal weakens. Information scatters.

People respond to this whether they are aware of it or not. They may not know why they feel calm around you. They may not be able to explain why they trust you quickly, why conversations flow, or why opportunities seem to arise in your presence. They're not responding to your words alone. They're responding to your coherence.

This is why presence matters more than performance. This is why authenticity carries more weight than effort. Your energy is not something you "send out" consciously. It's something you generate automatically based on how regulated and aligned your system is.

Energy is not just mystical. It's informational. And manifestation doesn't respond to what you say you want. It responds to the information your system is consistently broadcasting.

The Role of Repetition in Rewiring Reality

Repetition is how the brain decides what matters. Your nervous system is not persuaded by intensity or one powerful moment. It's persuaded by consistency. One emotional experience can open a door, but it doesn't rebuild the house. Identity is not rewritten by a breakthrough alone. It's rewritten by what happens next, and then next again.

Repeated emotional experiences are what tell the brain: *This is who we are now*. When a thought, a feeling, or a behavior shows up once, the brain treats it as an exception. When it shows up again and again, especially in a regulated state, the brain begins to treat it as truth.

This is why the 24/7 Manifestation Method emphasizes daily practice, morning and night repetition, embodied affirmation, and consistent check-ins. These aren't arbitrary rituals. They are exposure.

They give your system repeated evidence that a new way of being is safe, familiar, and reliable.

You are not trying to convince yourself with logic or force belief into place. You are training your system the same way it learned everything else, through repetition in real time. Just as physical training builds muscle through consistent stress and recovery, repetition builds identity through steady, embodied practice. Over time, what once felt unfamiliar becomes normal. And normal is where change sticks.

Energy Leaks: The Hidden Places Your Signal Gets Diluted

An energy leak is anywhere your attention, emotion, or life force is being drained in a way that contradicts what you're trying to build. It's not about doing something "wrong." It's about losing coherence. You can have a clear intention and still feel stuck if your energy is quietly bleeding out through habits, patterns, and reactions you've normalized.

An energy leak isn't always dramatic. In fact, the most powerful ones are subtle. They live in the background of daily life. They show up as small compromises, repeated distractions, emotional loops, and unexamined obligations. Each one pulls a little bit of charge away from your system. And over time, that dilution matters.

Here are where some of the most common places energy leaks occur:

- **People-pleasing:** Saying yes when your body says no. Managing other people's emotions at the expense of your own alignment.
- **Doomscrolling:** Consuming information that dysregulates your nervous system and fragments your attention.
- **Overcommitting:** Filling your calendar with obligations that leave no space for integration, rest, or clarity.
- **Self-judgment:** Running a constant internal commentary about what you should be doing better.
- **Drama cycles:** Replaying the same conversations, conflicts, or stories without resolution.

- **Avoidance:** Delaying decisions, conversations, or actions that require presence and courage.
- **Proving energy:** Acting from the need to justify your worth instead of trusting it.
- **Unfinished business:** Carrying mental tabs for things you've postponed, ignored, or left incomplete.

None of these mean you're failing. They mean your signal is scattered.

Here's the key distinction: manifestation is not just about adding new practices. It's also about reducing unnecessary drain. You can increase intention all you want, but if your energy is constantly leaking, the system never builds enough charge to create momentum.

You can't amplify a signal you keep leaking.

This is why some people feel like they're "doing everything right" and still not seeing movement. Their intention is clear, but their attention is divided. Their desire is real, but their energy is tied up in managing, avoiding, proving, or coping. The goal here is not perfection. It's awareness. When you start noticing where your energy goes unconsciously, you regain choice. And when choice returns, coherence strengthens.

In the chapters ahead, we'll talk about how to gently seal these leaks without force or self-criticism. For now, simply notice. Where does your energy feel clean and focused? And where does it quietly drain away? That noticing alone begins to change the signal.

Memory, Meaning, and Why the Past Keeps Repeating

One of the most misunderstood aspects of manifestation is the idea that the past is "over."

Chronologically, yes. Neurologically and emotionally, not always.

Your brain does not store memories like a filing cabinet where events are neatly archived and left alone. It stores them as living networks of sensation, emotion, meaning, and response. A memory is not just something that happened. It's a pattern your body learned from what happened. And that pattern continues to influence how you interpret the present until it is updated.

Every time a memory is recalled, it doesn't simply replay. It reactivates. The body re-enters the emotional and physiological state associated with that experience. And when a memory is reactivated, it becomes editable.

This process is called memory reconsolidation. It means the past is not as fixed as it feels. Beliefs formed during moments of shock, loss, humiliation, or fear are not permanent truths. They are conclusions your nervous system made in order to survive. And those conclusions can be revised when the body is given a new experience of safety alongside the old memory.

This is why simply understanding your patterns doesn't always free you from them. You can know exactly where a belief came from and still feel hijacked by it. Insight alone doesn't rewrite emotional memory. Experience does. Specifically, repeated experiences that pair awareness with regulation, intention with safety, and choice with embodiment.

The 24/7 Manifestation Method works at this deeper level. By pairing intention with emotion, repetition, and a regulated nervous system, you are not just learning something new intellectually. You are updating the meaning your body assigns to old experiences. You are teaching your system that what once felt dangerous is no longer happening now.

And when meaning changes, behavior changes. When behavior changes, your identity shifts. And when identity shifts, reality follows. Not because the past disappeared, but because it no longer gets to decide your future.

Why Identity Is the Master Switch

Identity is the set of assumptions you hold about who you are and how life works for you. It's the quiet narrative running underneath your choices, reactions, and expectations. Often, it sounds like familiar phrases you don't even question anymore: "I'm the kind of person who always has to try harder," or "I'm not someone who gets lucky," or "This is just how I am."

Your brain is deeply loyal to identity. Its primary job is consistency, not happiness. So, if your identity includes struggle, your behavior will unconsciously organize itself to maintain that story.

You may work harder than necessary, tolerate less than you deserve, or dismiss opportunities that contradict what feels "like you." Not because you want to stay stuck, but because consistency feels safer than change.

If your identity shifts to "I am capable," your behavior begins to align naturally. You take different actions without forcing them. You recover faster from setbacks. You stop over-explaining and start trusting your own decisions. This doesn't happen through willpower. Willpower fights the system. Identity leads it.

The fastest way to change behavior is not to demand more discipline, but to update the identity the behavior is protecting. And identity doesn't change through declarations alone. It changes through repeated action that feels safe, emotional experiences that reinforce a new self-concept, and consistent reinforcement over time. That is exactly what this method provides. Not a new personality to perform, but a new internal agreement about who you are allowed to be.

Why the Body Resists Unfamiliar Goodness

Here's something almost no one tells you about growth: your body can resist good things just as strongly as it resists danger. Not because something is wrong with you, but because of how the nervous system is designed. The nervous system is not oriented toward pleasure, success, or expansion. It is oriented toward predictability. Its primary question is not "Will this make me happy?" but "Have we survived this before?"

If chaos was familiar in your early life, calm can feel unsettling, even suspicious. If struggle was normalized, ease can feel undeserved or temporary. If love once led to loss, closeness could register as risk. These reactions are not conscious decisions. They are reflexes built through experience.

So, when you begin manifesting something new, you may expect excitement, relief, or joy. Instead, you notice something else. A tightening in your chest instead of expansion. Hesitation where you thought there would be certainty. A subtle urge to delay, deflect, or sabotage just as things begin to move. This is often the moment people assume they don't really want what they've been asking for.

But that's rarely true.

What's happening is simpler and more human: your body hasn't learned yet that it's safe to receive this. The nervous system is encountering something unfamiliar and responding with caution. Not to stop you, but to protect you.

Manifestation accelerates when safety is prioritized over speed. When the body feels rushed, it resists. When it feels included, it cooperates. That's why this method does not push you past your nervous system or demand that you override it. It brings the body with you, teaching it gradually that expansion does not equal danger. And when the body agrees, receiving becomes natural instead of forced.

Receiving Is a Skill (Not a Trait)

Many people believe receiving is something you're either naturally good at or inherently bad at. You either know how to accept love, support, or abundance, or you don't. But that belief misses something essential. Receiving is not a personality trait. It's a learned capacity.

If, early in life, asking led to disappointment, rejection, or ridicule, your nervous system adapted. If relying on others felt unsafe or unreliable, you learned to depend only on yourself. If independence was the way you stayed protected, then receiving may now feel exposed, uncomfortable, or even wrong. These patterns don't mean you're ungrateful or closed off. They mean your system learned how to survive.

This is why some people successfully manifest opportunities, only to struggle when they arrive. You might call in support, then immediately downplay it. You might receive abundance, then unconsciously leak it through chaos, over-giving, or guilt. You might be offered love and instinctively look for the exit. Not because you don't want it, but because your capacity to receive hasn't caught up to what you're calling in.

This is not a moral failure. It's not a mindset issue. It's a capacity issue.

The 24/7 Manifestation Method builds receiving capacity slowly and intentionally. It does not overwhelm the nervous system with sudden expansion. It introduces safety, repetition, and regulation so your system can learn that receiving does not equal danger or loss of control. And when receiving feels safe, what you've been asking for no longer slips through your fingers.

Why Environment Is a Subconscious Signal

Your environment is constantly communicating with your nervous system, whether you realize it or not. Every object, pile, sound, and unfinished task sends a signal. Clutter whispers: *There is unfinished business.* Chaos suggests: *There is no containment here.* And environments with a sense of order quietly say: *You are safe now.*

This isn't about perfection or aesthetics. It's about coherence. Your nervous system reads your surroundings as information. When your space feels overwhelming, crowded, or unresolved, your body often stays in a low-grade state of alert. When your space feels intentional and supported, your system can relax just enough to expand.

This is why small environmental shifts often come before big internal or external changes. Clearing a drawer. Making your bed. Letting go of something you've been meaning to fix "someday." These actions aren't trivial. They are signals. They tell your subconscious that things can be completed, that there is room, that you are capable of holding order and care.

You're not just cleaning or organizing. You're teaching your system how to hold more clarity, more ease, and more responsibility without overwhelm. When your outer world begins to match your inner intention, the signal becomes clear. And clear signals create momentum.

Identity Shifts Happen in Ordinary Moments

Identity doesn't change in one grand declaration or dramatic breakthrough. It changes quietly, almost imperceptibly, through repetition. Through the moments no one applauds. Through the choices that feel small but are deeply corrective. Identity is shaped in how you live, not in what you announce.

When you choose rest instead of proving your worth, you send your system a new message about safety. When you tell the truth instead of performing, you teach your body that authenticity will not cost you belonging. When you set a boundary without over-explaining, you reinforce the belief that your needs are valid. When you follow through on something small, especially when it would be easier to abandon it, you build trust with yourself.

Each of these moments sends a signal: *This is who I am now*. Not as an aspiration, but as a lived experience. The brain listens for patterns, not promises. The nervous system adjusts to what is repeated, not what is imagined. And reality responds accordingly. Over time, these quiet shifts accumulate. What once felt effortful becomes natural. What once felt unfamiliar becomes normal. That's how identity truly changes.

A Simple Embodiment Practice

Before continuing, pause for a moment. Let this chapter settle instead of rushing past it. Place one hand on your heart and one on your belly, feeling the warmth and weight of your own presence. Take five slow, intentional breaths, allowing each exhale to soften your shoulders and jaw. With each inhale, notice the subtle rise of your body. Then say quietly, either out loud or internally: *My body is learning something new*. Don't analyze the words. Don't try to feel anything specific. Simply notice what happens. A sensation. A breath shift. A sense of grounding. That noticing is embodiment.

What This Means for Your Manifestation

You are not manifesting from your thoughts alone, no matter how intentional or positive they may be. You are manifesting from the state your entire system is in. From your nervous system, which decides whether something feels safe or threatening. From your habitual patterns, which quietly dictate what you repeat without thinking. From your embodied identity, the version of yourself your body already recognizes as familiar. And from your energetic coherence, the degree to which all these parts are working together instead of pulling in different directions.

This isn't complicated, but it is precise. Manifestation doesn't require more effort or better thoughts. It requires alignment across systems. When those systems agree, change becomes sustainable. When they don't, progress feels inconsistent or exhausting.

Once you understand this, manifestation stops feeling mystical or unpredictable and starts feeling practical. You can see why certain patterns repeat and why others dissolve. Up to now, you've been introduced to the architecture: brain, body, and field. Next, we're going to explore why the past keeps resurfacing even when your conscious mind wants something new, and how to update those patterns without force, pressure, or self-blame.

Why Manifestation Often Looks Ordinary at First

One of the biggest disappointments people experience with manifestation is expecting it to arrive dramatically. Fireworks. Announcements. Instant certainty. A clear moment where everything changes at once and you *know* it worked. When that doesn't happen, people assume they've missed something or done it wrong.

But real transformation rarely announces itself. It usually moves quietly, beneath the surface, long before anything visible shifts. It shows up as clearer decisions that don't require hours of debate. Steadier emotions that no longer swing so violently. Faster recovery when you're triggered instead of spiraling for days. Less overthinking. More follow-through on small promises to yourself.

These changes can feel underwhelming at first because they don't look like miracles. But they're not minor. They are structural. They change how your system operates day to day. And when the structure changes, results follow naturally. External manifestations aren't sudden arrivals. They're the inevitable outcome of an internal system that's finally organized to receive them.

The Role of Synchronicity (Without Losing Grounding)

As alignment increases, many people begin to notice signs and synchronicities showing up in their lives. Repeating numbers on clocks or receipts. Unexpected messages that arrive at just the right moment. Chance meetings that open doors you weren't actively looking for. "Wrong turns" that end up leading somewhere unexpectedly right.

These moments can feel magical, but they're not rewards for doing manifestation correctly. They're feedback. They reflect a system that's becoming more coherent, more responsive, more awake. When your internal state begins to stabilize, your perception sharpens. You notice patterns you might have missed before. You're more receptive. More present. More available for connection and opportunity.

Synchronicities help reinforce belief during the space between intention and outcome. They remind you that movement is happening even when the final result hasn't arrived yet. The key, though, is not to hand over your power to signs. They're not instructions. They're confirmations. They're meant to support your agency, not replace it.

The 24/7 Manifestation Method keeps you grounded in action and responsibility while still honoring mystery. You stay rooted in choice, while allowing life to meet you in meaningful ways.

Closing: Rewiring Through Repetition

Your brain rewires through repetition.

Your nervous system expands through safety.

Your energy field coheres through alignment.

When these systems work together, manifestation stops feeling fragile or hit-or-miss. It becomes stable. Reliable. Sustainable. Not because you've finally cracked some secret code or learned how to "do it right," but because your internal world is no longer working against itself.

This is what congruence really means. Your thoughts are no longer arguing with your body. Your desires are no longer fighting your nervous system. Your actions are no longer canceling out your intentions. When your internal systems agree, reality responds naturally. Not as a reward, but as a reflection.

You are not trying to manifest a new life by force. You are not chasing outcomes or attempting to override who you are. You are becoming the version of yourself for whom that life makes sense. The version who can hold it. Sustain it. Live inside it without self-sabotage or collapse.

That becoming doesn't happen in one dramatic moment. It happens quietly and consistently:

In your breath, when you choose regulation instead of panic.

In your body, when you listen instead of override.

In your choices, when you respond instead of react.

In your environment, when you create space for what you're calling in.

In your identity, when you begin to act from who you are becoming rather than who you've been.

This is real change. It is change that lasts because it's built into your system, not layered on top of it.

In the next chapter, we'll move from understanding into practice. We'll break down the Four Pillars that support this entire method and show you how to live them in real time, in ordinary days, not ideal conditions.

For now, pause.

Let your system integrate what it's learned.

Notice what feels different, even subtly. You are learning how to change in a way that lasts.

Reflection Questions

1. What feels unfamiliar but aligned in your life right now?
2. Where does your body tighten when you imagine receiving?
3. What belief is ready to be updated?
4. What small action would signal safety to your nervous system today?

Answer honestly.
Progress doesn't require perfection.

PART II

The Steps for Implementing the 24/7 Manifestation Method

CHAPTER 4

The 24/7 Manifestation Blueprint

How to Live in Alignment All Day, Every Day

There comes a moment in every real transformation when understanding is no longer enough.

You've read the books. You've nodded along. You've had the realizations that felt like they should have changed everything. And yet, your life hasn't fully caught up.

That gap is not a failure. It's not a lack of discipline, belief, or effort. It's the moment when insight is asking to become embodied. Because information can inspire you, but it cannot rewire you. Knowing something is true is very different from living as if it's true, especially when you're tired, triggered, busy, or overwhelmed.

This chapter exists for that exact moment.

This is where manifestation moves out of theory and into practice, out of peak experiences and into ordinary days, and out of concepts you understand and into patterns you live. Here, alignment is no longer something you reach for when you need something. It becomes the way you start your mornings, the way you respond when your energy dips, the way you make decisions under pressure, and the way you close your day when no one is watching.

This chapter is about integration, about creating a rhythm that holds you even when motivation fades, and about making alignment automatic instead of effortful. This is where manifestation stops being something you do once in a while and starts becoming something you are.

Welcome to the Blueprint of the 24/7 Manifestation Method.

Why You Need a Blueprint (Not More Motivation)

Most people approach manifestation the same way they approach fitness.

They wait until they feel motivated. They go all in for a few days or weeks.

They feel good, inspired, committed. And then life gets busy, energy dips, something unexpected happens, and the practice quietly falls away.

Not because they don't care. But because motivation was never meant to carry something long term.

Manifestation doesn't respond to intensity. It responds to consistency. It responds to what you repeat when no one is watching, not what you do during a surge of inspiration. This is why so many people feel like manifestation "works" for a moment and then stops. They were relying on emotional momentum instead of structural support.

You don't need to be high vibe all the time. You don't need perfect thoughts.

You don't need to control your emotions or override your humanity.

You need a structure that holds you steady when motivation fades. You need a system that works on tired days, neutral days, messy days, and ordinary days. That's what a blueprint provides.

A blueprint removes guesswork. It tells you what to do when your mind feels scattered. It gives your nervous system something familiar to return to when emotions fluctuate. It creates continuity so that even on imperfect days, your energy is still moving in the same direction.

The 24/7 Manifestation Method isn't about adding more to your life. It's about bringing alignment into what you're already doing. When structure supports your system, consistency becomes natural. And when consistency is in place, manifestation stops feeling fragile and starts becoming reliable.

Manifestation Is Not a Moment; It's a Rhythm

Your life is not created by your biggest moments. It's created by your patterns.

Not the breakthrough conversation. Not the inspired decision you make once. Not the day everything finally feels clear.

Your reality is shaped by what you repeat:

How you start your day when no one is watching

How you respond when something doesn't go as planned

How you speak to yourself internally when you're tired, triggered, or unsure

How you close your day and what your nervous system carries into sleep

These moments may feel small, but they are powerful because they repeat. And repetition is what programs the subconscious. The brain doesn't change based on what you understand. It changes based on what you practice. The nervous system doesn't reorganize around intention. It reorganizes around rhythm.

That's why this method is built around four daily touchpoints that create energetic coherence throughout your entire day:

Morning Alignment

Midday Check-in

Inspired Action

Evening Integration

These are not tasks to complete or boxes to check. They are energetic anchors. They bring you back into alignment again and again, so your frequency stays consistent even when life is not. When your day has structure, your system has stability. And stability is what allows real change to take root.

The Four Daily Anchors of the 24/7 Manifestation Method

There are four daily anchors to the 24/7 Manifestation Method.

MORNING ALIGNMENT: SETTING THE FREQUENCY

The first moments of your day matter more than you realize.

Before emails.

Before social media.

Before conversations, responsibilities, or other people's expectations enter your field.

This is the window where your subconscious is most impressionable. Your nervous system is still orienting itself. Your brain is moving out of sleep. Your body is deciding what kind of day it's about to live inside of. Morning alignment is not about hype or positivity. It's about orientation.

In the 24/7 Manifestation Method, morning alignment is where you set the frequency your system will reference for the rest of the day. Writing your affirmation 24 times is not about convincing yourself of anything. It's repetition with presence. It tells your brain, *this matters*. Visualization is not about fantasizing wildly. It's about choosing one grounded, believable scene from your desired reality and letting your body feel what normal would feel like there. When you choose one emotional state to embody, you're not demanding happiness. You're choosing familiarity. Calm. Confidence. Trust. Ease.

Asking, "What would my future self do first today?" immediately moves you out of reaction and into identity. You're not forcing belief. You're planting familiarity. You're teaching your brain, gently and consistently: "This is the direction we're going."

MIDDAY CHECK-IN: STAYING IN ALIGNMENT

Alignment is not static. Energy shifts. Life happens.

The goal is not to stay "high vibe." The goal is to notice drift and return without judgment. This is where most manifestation methods break down. They focus heavily on the beginning and the end of the day and ignore the middle, where real life happens.

The midday check-in is a pause, not a performance. And pause does not mean you need to leave your desk, find a quiet room, or stop your day completely. It simply means creating a brief moment of awareness.

You can do it wherever you are. Sitting at your desk. Walking to your car. Standing in your kitchen. In between meetings. In the middle of a conversation, even. This is not about removing yourself from your life. It is about returning to yourself within it.

You can ask the questions silently in your mind or write them down if that feels supportive. There is no perfect way to do this. The only goal is to become aware.

It's where you ask simple but powerful questions:

How does my body feel right now?

What emotion am I broadcasting?

Am I acting from my future self or my fear self?

This moment matters because it interrupts autopilot. Without it, one email, one comment, one delay can hijack your nervous system for hours. With it, you recalibrate instead of spiral. Even 30 seconds of awareness can reroute the entire rest of your day. This is not about fixing yourself because you are not broken to begin with. It's simply about noticing and choosing again.

INSPIRED ACTION: MOVING WITHOUT FORCE

Manifestation requires movement, but not hustle, not pressure, not proving. Inspired action comes from alignment, not urgency. It feels clear. Grounded. Slightly stretchy, but not overwhelming.

This blueprint teaches you how to recognize the difference between action driven by fear and action guided by alignment. Fear-based action feels frantic and heavy. It's fueled by "shoulds" and timelines. Inspired action feels intentional. It often looks small: One email. One conversation. One boundary. One moment of rest instead of pushing.

You don't need to do everything. You need to do the next aligned thing. That's how timelines shift. Not through force, but through consistency rooted in identity.

EVENING INTEGRATION: LOCKING IT IN

Your day doesn't end when you stop working. It ends when your nervous system decides what to store. Evening integration is where meaning is assigned. What you review before sleep becomes the template your subconscious works with overnight.

Writing your affirmation 24 times before bed, again reinforces identity. Reflecting on one sign, one win, or one aligned moment trains your brain to notice support. Gratitude signals safety. Closing the day with regulation instead of stimulation tells your system it's safe to rest.

You're not reviewing your failures.

You're training your subconscious to expect alignment.

And that expectation is powerful.

Morning Alignment: Why Writing Comes First

You might be wondering why this method emphasizes writing instead of relying only on visualization or spoken affirmations. It's not because those tools don't work. It's because writing engages your system more completely. Writing does three critical things at once: it slows the mind, it engages the body, and it activates repetition with focused attention. That combination is powerful.

When you write an affirmation by hand, you are involving multiple systems simultaneously. Cognitive processing shapes the meaning of the words. Motor movement brings the body into participation. Sensory feedback grounds the experience in the present moment. Together, these layers create a much stronger neurological signal than passive repetition alone. Your brain registers writing as effortful, intentional, and important.

Writing communicates something very specific to your nervous system: "This matters enough to pause for. This is worth my attention." And attention is what tells the brain what to prioritize.

When this practice is done in the hypnagogic window, right after waking or just before sleep, it bypasses the analytical mind almost entirely. You are not debating with doubt. You are not trying to convince yourself. You are quietly installing a new default, one repetition at a time.

The Six Core Tools That Make the Method Work

The 24/7 Manifestation Method works because it is supported by six core tools that operate together to rewire your subconscious, regulate your nervous system, and align your identity with the reality you're calling in. These tools are not separate techniques you use once in a while. They are integrated supports that shape how you think, feel, act, and respond every day.

Quantum visualization is a full-body rehearsal of your future self. It is not daydreaming. By repeatedly visualizing specific moments from your desired reality and emotionally inhabiting them, you train your brain and nervous system to recognize that future as familiar and safe.

Emotional recalibration teaches you how to shift your internal state without bypassing what you feel. Through breath, movement, sound, or presence, you learn to process emotion so that it no longer hijacks your behavior or blocks expansion.

Language alchemy works with the power of words to shape belief and behavior. Writing affirmations in present tense, especially during morning and night windows, rewires inner dialogue and creates new subconscious defaults.

Identity activation is the practice of becoming. You don't manifest what you want. You manifest who you are. This tool helps you make decisions, set boundaries, and take action from your future self now.

Rituals that rewire create rhythm. Repetition turns intention into habit, habit into identity, and identity into reality. Ritual is how change becomes embodied.

Energetic architecture protects and refines your field. What you allow in, conversations, content, environments, shapes your internal world. This tool teaches you to guard your energy so coherence can build.

Together, these tools turn manifestation into a lived system, not a fleeting practice.

The Seven-day Focus Cycle

The blueprint unfolds over seven days, each with a specific energetic focus.

Seven isn't magic, though it is deeply symbolic across cultures and systems.

But seven days is long enough to build momentum and short enough to stay present, engaged, and willing. This is not about intensity. It is about continuity.

Each day builds on the last, creating a progressive shift in awareness, regulation, and identity.

DAY 1: SET THE INTENTION

Clarity creates power. When the mind knows where it is going, the nervous system can begin to orient. Vague desires scatter energy. Clear intention organizes it.

DAY 2: ASSIGN YOUR SIGN

Belief needs reinforcement. Signs are not proof. They are feedback that keeps the system engaged during the gap between intention and result.

DAY 3: CHECK YOUR ENERGY

Awareness precedes change. You cannot shift patterns you are not willing to see. This day builds honest observation without self-judgment.

DAY 4: THE 100 WAYS EXERCISE

Detachment expands possibility. Releasing attachment to how something must happen opens the field dramatically.

DAY 5: TRUST THE PROCESS

Trust is not passive. It is a regulated state. Faith stabilizes the nervous system when results have not arrived yet.

DAY 6: STRENGTH IN COMMUNITY

Witnessing anchors belief. Being seen and supported reinforces what the mind alone struggles to hold.

DAY 7: INTEGRATION

Identity locks in change. This is where repetition turns insight into embodiment.

You are not finishing after seven days.

You are installing a new operating system that continues to run long after the week ends.

A Story of Alignment in Motion

One of the most common things I hear from people who use this blueprint is, "I didn't even realize my life was changing until I looked back."

They're often surprised by that. They expected a moment. A breakthrough. A clear line where everything shifted. Instead, the change crept in quietly. Decisions felt easier. Emotional reactions softened. Old patterns stopped running the show. Life felt more manageable, more spacious, more intentional.

That's because coherence doesn't arrive with fireworks. It arrives as steadiness. And steadiness is powerful. When your nervous system is regulated and your energy is consistent, change doesn't need to announce itself. It integrates. And integration is what lasts.

Living the Blueprint on Ordinary Days

Here's the thing no one tells you about manifestation. The days that matter most are not the days when you feel inspired, expansive, or crystal-clear. Those days are easy. Your mind cooperates. Your energy feels open. Your future self feels close enough to touch.

The days that shape your reality are the ordinary ones. The ones where life is still life.

The days that matter most are different:

The days you're tired

The days nothing obvious is happening

The days you feel neutral, bored, or slightly off

The days you're tempted to say, "I'll start again tomorrow"

Those are the days your nervous system defaults to its old training. Those are the days your subconscious tests whether this new way of being is real or just a phase. So, they abandon the practice, not because it isn't working, but because it isn't entertaining.

But neutrality is not absence.

It's incubation.

Incubation is the quiet space where internal change is organizing itself before it becomes visible. It's where your brain is building new pathways. It's where your body is learning that steady is safe. It's where your identity is adjusting behind the scenes. And if you can stay consistent during incubation, the shift completes.

That's why this blueprint was designed for real life, not retreat life. Manifestation mastery isn't about peak moments. It's about what you practice when nothing dramatic is happening. When your feelings aren't perfect. When your energy dips. When you don't get instant feedback.

The blueprint keeps you aligned during incubation, so you don't sabotage what's forming just because it's quiet.

Now that you've seen the four anchors, let's slow down and walk through what each one is really doing inside your brain and body.

THE SEVEN-DAY ARC: WHAT EACH DAY BUILDS

Let's revisit the seven-day focus cycle through the lens of what it's actually doing inside your system. This arc isn't random, and it's not just a sequence of themes. Each day builds a specific layer of coherence, so by the end of the week, your brain, body, and identity are all pointing in the same direction.

DAY 1: INTENTION

Clarity organizes energy. When a desire is vague, the subconscious has nothing to orient toward, so your actions scatter and your nervous system stays uncertain. Day 1 gives your system a clear destination. Specificity tells your brain, *this matters*, and gives your body something concrete to feel into.

DAY 2: SIGN

Belief needs reinforcement, especially before results arrive. Assigning a sign keeps your nervous system engaged during the gap between intention and manifestation. It provides feedback without pressure, reminding your system that movement is happening even when outcomes aren't visible yet.

DAY 3: ENERGY CHECK

You cannot change what you do not notice. This day builds awareness without judgment. Instead of fixing or forcing, you observe where resistance, fear, or contraction lives. Awareness alone begins to loosen patterns because the body feels seen rather than overridden.

DAY 4: 100 WAYS

Attachment to *how* constricts possibility. This exercise deliberately expands the field, teaching your brain to release control and your nervous system to tolerate uncertainty without panic. Possibility widens, and pressure dissolves.

DAY 5: TRUST

Trust is not passive. It's an active state of safety. This day stabilizes the nervous system so that it doesn't collapse into doubt when results haven't arrived yet.

DAY 6: COMMUNITY

Witnessing strengthens belief. You are not meant to do this alone. Community isn't just encouragement. It's nervous system evidence. When you're witnessed in your becoming, your new identity feels real, and the old one loses authority.

DAY 7: INTEGRATION

This is where identity locks in. Through repetition and reflection, the work stops being something you're doing and starts becoming who you are.

A STORY OF INTEGRATION

One woman shared with me that by Day 7, she felt "different, but couldn't explain why." Nothing dramatic had happened on the surface. There was no big breakthrough moment or obvious external win. But inside, something fundamental had shifted. Her reactions had softened. Situations that would normally spike anxiety or frustration felt easier to move through. Her self-talk was quieter, kinder, less urgent. She noticed she was more patient with herself, less demanding, less critical, and more trusting of her own timing.

That's integration.

Manifestation doesn't always announce itself with fireworks or instant results. Often, it arrives as a subtle sense of steadiness. A calm where there used to be tension. A pause where there used to be panic. And that peace is not the end result. It's the doorway. When peace becomes your baseline, everything else has room to arrive.

When You Miss a Day (And You Will)

Let's be clear: missing a day does not undo your progress. This work is not fragile, and neither are you. The 24/7 Manifestation Blueprint was never designed for perfection. It's not about never falling out of alignment. It's about knowing how to return without punishment or drama.

When you miss a ritual, you don't spiral. You don't question whether the method works. You don't tell yourself a story about failure. You simply come back. No guilt. No self-lecture. No starting over from zero. Return itself is the practice.

Every time you return, you strengthen the pathway. Every repair builds trust with your nervous system. Every moment of self-compassion reinforces your identity as someone who stays with themselves. The blueprint is resilient by design. And the more you practice returning, the more resilient you become too.

How the Blueprint Stabilizes Your Nervous System

As we touched on earlier, your nervous system plays a central role in what you are able to hold, receive, and sustain. But here, we begin to understand how that actually stabilizes in practice.

Your nervous system loves rhythm. It is constantly looking for patterns it can rely on, cues that tell it what to expect next. Predictable anchors signal safety. And safety is what allows expansion to occur without resistance.

When your system knows what's coming, it stops scanning for danger and starts allocating energy toward growth. The background tension begins to ease. You stop bracing for the unknown. The nervous system no longer has to stay on high alert because there is structure it can trust.

This is why people often report feeling calmer within the first few days of the 24/7 Manifestation Method, even before anything external has shifted.

No money has arrived yet.

No opportunity has landed.

No dramatic breakthrough has occurred.

And yet, internally, something has changed. Stability has returned. That stability isn't passive. It's active containment. It's the feeling that your system can hold what's coming without being overwhelmed.

A nervous system that feels safe becomes receptive.

It becomes flexible, open, capable of receiving support, opportunity, and ease without immediately pushing them away. Nothing external has changed yet. But internally, the foundation has been laid. And stability is the foundation of receiving.

CHOOSING THE RIGHT AFFIRMATION

Your affirmation should feel expansive enough to invite growth, but believable enough that your body doesn't reject it. It should activate possibility without triggering defense. It should point toward desire, not spotlight what's missing. This is subtle, but essential. An affirmation that sounds impressive but causes your system to brace will slow progress, not accelerate it.

A simple way to test your language is to notice your body while you write. Does your breath soften or tighten? Do your shoulders drop or creep upward? Does your chest feel open or guarded? Your nervous system will answer before your mind does. If you feel tension, resistance, or irritation, that's not failure. It's information.

When that happens, adjust the language until your body can stay present. Safety always comes first. Growth cannot bypass it.

For example, instead of declaring, "I am wildly wealthy," you might begin with, "I am learning to feel safe receiving more." That statement still moves you forward, but it does so without overwhelming your system. And often, those gentler, truer statements create far more lasting change than bold declarations your body isn't ready to hold yet.

Midday Alignment: Interrupting Autopilot

The midpoint of your day is often where old patterns quietly reclaim control. Emails pile up. Conversations carry unexpected charge. Fatigue sets in. Without awareness, your nervous system defaults to what's familiar, and the rest of the day begins running on autopilot. You may not notice the shift, but it shows up in your tone, your decisions, and your reactions.

The midday check-in exists to interrupt that loop before it hardens. It creates a pause between stimulus and response. In that pause, you ask a powerful question: *Am I responding from my past or my future?* Not as a judgment, but as an orientation point.

This moment isn't about fixing your mood or forcing positivity. It's about restoring choice. Choice brings agency back online. Agency returns a sense of internal power. Even a brief pause, 30 seconds of breath, sensation, or awareness, can reroute your nervous system and shift the trajectory of your entire afternoon.

A STORY OF MIDDAY REALIGNMENT

I once worked with a woman who described herself as "highly reactive." She didn't say it with drama or self-pity. It was simply how she understood herself. Every small disruption derailed her: A delayed email. A comment that felt sharp. A change in plans. Her nervous system went immediately into alert, and once it did, the rest of her day felt unpredictable and exhausting.

She wasn't lacking discipline or insight. She had read the books. She knew her patterns. But knowing didn't stop her body from reacting. Through the 24/7 Manifestation Method, she didn't try to become calmer or more positive. She committed to one simple midday ritual. When she noticed herself tipping into reactivity, she would place her feet flat on the floor, slow her breath, and ask a single question: "What do I need right now to stay aligned?"

Sometimes the answer was water. Sometimes it was standing up and moving her body. Sometimes it was setting a boundary or stepping away from a conversation that was pulling her out of herself. The power wasn't in the action. It was in the pause. The pause returned choice.

Within two weeks, she said something that stayed with me: "I feel like I'm driving my life again instead of being dragged through it." Nothing in her external circumstances had changed yet. The same responsibilities were there. The same people. The same pressures. But her relationship to herself had shifted. She was responding instead of reacting. And that changed everything.

INSPIRED ACTION: THE DIFFERENCE BETWEEN FORCE AND FLOW

Inspired action is often misunderstood. People assume it means sitting back, waiting for a lightning bolt of motivation or a perfectly timed sign from the universe. They imagine that if it's truly aligned, it should feel exciting, obvious, or effortless from the start. That's not how it works.

Inspired action is quieter than that. It doesn't rush you, and it doesn't pressure you. It feels intentional, grounded, and clear. It arises from presence rather than panic, from listening rather than forcing. Most of the time, it looks surprisingly small: One email you've been postponing. One honest conversation. One decision you've been circling around because it felt uncomfortable to face.

What matters is not the size of the action, but the state it comes from. Fear-based action carries urgency. It feels tight, reactive, and charged with the need to fix or prove something. Inspired action, by contrast, feels steady. There is movement, but not desperation. Direction, but not force.

This blueprint teaches you how to recognize that difference in your body, so you stop mistaking anxiety for intuition and alignment for inaction.

WHY SMALL ACTIONS CREATE BIG SHIFTS

Your nervous system trusts consistency far more than intensity. It doesn't need grand gestures or dramatic leaps to feel safe. In fact, those often trigger the opposite response. A small action taken from alignment sends a powerful signal inward. It reinforces identity by proving, "This is who I am now." It builds self-trust because you follow through without forcing. And it strengthens coherence, allowing your thoughts, emotions, and behavior to stay in conversation with each other.

Large, forced actions can look impressive on the outside, but internally they often create backlash. The system tightens. Resistance grows. Burnout follows shortly after. That's why this method prioritizes micro-movements, repeated daily, from a regulated state. These actions feel manageable, even on hard days. Over time, momentum builds quietly, almost invisibly. And then, seemingly all at once, life responds.

Evening Integration: Where Manifestation Accelerates

Most people underestimate the power of how they end their day, focusing far more on what they do in the morning or how productive they were in the afternoon. But from a neurological and energetic standpoint, night is just as influential, if not more so. As you prepare for sleep, the conscious mind softens and the subconscious comes forward. This is the moment when your brain is deciding what to store, what to reinforce, and what to keep running in the background.

If you replay stress, frustration, or perceived failure, your subconscious treats those states as important. It rehearses them, strengthens them, and brings them forward into the next day. You don't wake up fresh. You wake up already carrying yesterday.

Evening integration changes that trajectory. When you intentionally anchor gratitude, notice evidence of alignment, or reflect on even one moment of safety or support, you send a very different signal. You teach your system, "This is what matters. This is what we're building." While you sleep, the subconscious works with that information, reorganizing around expansion instead of threat.

This isn't about pretending the day was perfect. It's about choosing what you feed your system last. Evening integration isn't a bonus or an optional add-on. It's the part that allows everything else to settle, consolidate, and stick.

THE ROLE OF GRATITUDE (WITHOUT BYPASSING)

Gratitude is not about pretending everything is perfect or forcing yourself into positivity when something feels hard. It's not spiritual bypassing, and it's not denial. Gratitude is a signal. It says to your nervous system, "I see what is working. I see what is supporting me right now." That single shift matters more than people realize.

Your nervous system is constantly scanning for threat or support. When attention is habitually placed on what's missing, wrong, or unresolved, the body stays in a low-grade state of vigilance. But when you intentionally notice moments of alignment, safety, or progress, even small ones, the system begins to relax. Relaxation creates capacity. Capacity allows expansion.

The brain repeats what it tracks. Whatever you consistently notice gets reinforced as important. When you track problems, you become skilled at finding them. When you track alignment, regulation, and support, those patterns strengthen. Gratitude isn't about ignoring reality. It's about training your system to recognize the parts of reality that are already working in your favor.

Making the Blueprint Yours

This is not a rigid system meant to be followed perfectly or performed exactly as written. It's a living framework designed to grow with you. As your nervous system stabilizes, as your identity shifts, and as your capacity to receive expands, the way you work with this blueprint will naturally evolve. That's not a sign you're doing it wrong. It's a sign you're doing it well.

As you move through this book, you'll begin to personalize the process in ways that feel intuitive and supportive. Your affirmations will change as your desires become clearer and your sense of self becomes more grounded. Your check-in rituals will adapt to your schedule, your seasons, and your emotional landscape. Your inspired actions will become subtler, more confident, and less driven by urgency. Your integration practices will deepen as regulation and reflection become familiar rather than forced.

What doesn't change is the structure. The rhythm remains. The anchors stay in place. That consistency is what gives your nervous system something to trust. Within that safety, expression is free to evolve.

Mastery is not about rigid adherence. It's about relationship—a relationship with your energy, your patterns, and your inner signals. When you can hold structure without constriction and flexibility without chaos, you are no longer following a method. You are living it. That's mastery.

A Day Inside the 24/7 Manifestation Blueprint

To truly understand this blueprint, it helps to see it lived.

Not on a perfect day.

Not on vacation.

Not on a retreat.

But on a regular, unremarkable day.

The kind of day that actually shapes your life.

So, let's walk through one.

You wake up and, before you reach for your phone, before the noise of the world rushes in, you sit up in bed. Your body is still warm with sleep. Your nervous system hasn't been pulled outward yet. Your mind is quiet enough to receive. This is a small window, but it matters.

You open your notebook and write your affirmation 24 times.

Not rushed.

Not multitasking.

Just present.

Maybe the affirmation is about confidence. Maybe it's about peace. Maybe it's about money, love, clarity, or trust. Whatever it is, it reflects the version of you that you are becoming. As you write, something subtle happens. Your breath slows. Your shoulders drop. Your energy begins to organize. You're not trying to feel anything dramatic. You're allowing familiarity to build.

Then you visualize one moment from your future. Not a highlight reel. Not a fantasy montage. A simple, grounded scene. You see yourself moving through it with ease. You feel the emotion of it, not excitement, but normalcy. Like this is already part of your life. That's morning alignment. You've set the frequency your system will reference all day.

Later, life happens. A message comes in. A delay throws off your schedule. A comment lands wrong. You feel the familiar tightening begin. This is where old patterns used to take over. But now, you pause. You ask, "Where is my energy right now?" You take one slow breath. You feel your feet on the floor. You choose a response instead of reacting. That's midday alignment. A small moment that changes the direction of the rest of your day.

Later still, you feel a nudge. It's not dramatic. Send the email. Clean the desk. Have the conversation. Or maybe rest instead of push. You take one small action, not because you're forcing progress, but because it feels aligned. That's inspired action.

At night, before sleep, you return to your notebook. You write your affirmation again. You note one moment of alignment, one sign, one win, one thing you're grateful for. You signal safety. You close the loop. That's evening integration.

Nothing dramatic happened.

And yet, everything moved.

That is the blueprint in action.

Why This Works Even When You Don't Feel Like It

One of the most powerful aspects of the 24/7 Manifestation Blueprint is that it works even when your motivation fluctuates. In fact, it's designed for those fluctuations. Motivation is emotional. It rises and falls based on sleep, stress, hormones, and circumstances. If manifestation depended on motivation, it would only work on your best days. But real change isn't built on your best days. It's built on the ordinary ones.

That's because motivation is not the driver. Regulation is.

You do not need to feel inspired to write your affirmation. You do not need to feel positive to pause and check in with your body. You do not need to feel confident to take the next aligned step. What you need is a rhythm your nervous system recognizes. When the body knows what to expect, it stops waiting for permission from mood and starts cooperating with structure.

Consistency is what trains the subconscious. It teaches your system what is normal. Consistency builds trust with your body because you are no longer abandoning yourself based on how you feel that day. Over time, that trust turns into stability. Stability turns into identity. And identity is what reality responds to.

This blueprint removes the emotional drama from manifestation. There is no need to chase a feeling or judge yourself for not being "in the right energy." Instead, you return to simple, repeatable anchors that keep your system coherent even when your emotions fluctuate. Alignment becomes less about how you feel and more about how you show up. And when coherence becomes steady, results stop feeling fragile. They last.

Manifestation as a Lifestyle, Not a Phase

Many people approach manifestation as something they do when they want something. A goal appears, a desire surfaces, and they reach for the tools. Then, once the urgency fades or life gets busy, the practice disappears. This method teaches something very different. It teaches you how to live in a way where alignment is your baseline, not a special effort. Awareness becomes automatic instead of forced. Self-trust is practiced daily through small, consistent choices. Regulation feels familiar rather than exceptional. And receiving no longer triggers fear or guilt because your nervous system knows it is safe.

When this becomes your lifestyle, manifestation stops feeling like work. You are no longer chasing outcomes or trying to get reality to respond. Your internal state does the inviting for you. Opportunities, connections, and clarity begin to meet you where you are. Manifestations stop being events you wait for and start becoming a natural consequence of how you live.

Let's talk about the space between intention and result. The gap.

This is where most people quietly abandon the process. They start to scan their reality for proof and come up empty. Nothing has "arrived" yet. No dramatic shift. No external confirmation. And the mind jumps in with familiar conclusions: *Nothing is happening. I must be doing it wrong. This doesn't work for me.*

But the gap is not a failure zone. It's a recalibration zone.

In this space, your nervous system is learning a new baseline. It's adjusting to unfamiliar levels of safety, expansion, and possibility.

Your identity is updating in subtle ways, releasing assumptions that no longer fit who you're becoming. Old patterns are loosening their grip, even if they haven't fully fallen away yet. And your energy field is reorganizing, shifting from scattered or reactive to more coherent and stable.

This stage often feels quiet, sometimes neutral, sometimes mildly uncomfortable. There may be less emotional charge than you expect, which can be confusing if you're used to intensity as a marker of progress. But neutrality is not stagnation. It's integration. It's the system doing deep work beneath the surface.

The danger of the gap is not that nothing is happening. It's that people interfere too soon. They overcorrect. They force. They quit. The 24/7 Manifestation Blueprint exists to hold you steady here. It keeps you anchored while the shift completes, so you don't sabotage what's already in motion.

Why This Method Doesn't Require Blind Faith

One of the reasons people trust the 24/7 Manifestation Method is because it doesn't ask for blind belief. It doesn't require you to convince yourself, override your doubts, or pretend you feel confident when you don't. It asks for participation. That's it. You don't need certainty. You don't need unwavering faith. You don't even need to feel optimistic. You need willingness—willingness to show up, to practice, and to engage honestly with where you are right now.

This matters because belief is unstable for most people. It fluctuates with mood, energy, and circumstance. Participation, on the other hand, builds evidence. Every time you engage with the process, your nervous system receives feedback: *I showed up. I stayed present. I followed through.* Over time, that evidence becomes trust. Not abstract trust in the universe, but embodied trust in yourself. Results don't come from doing it perfectly. They come from staying in relationship with the process long enough for your system to change.

That's why awareness is such a powerful starting point.

A QUICK INVENTORY: WHERE AM I BROADCASTING FROM?

Grab your journal and slow down for a moment. This is not about judgment. It's about clarity.

Circle the areas of life that feel most activated for you right now:

- Money
- Love
- Health
- Creative purpose
- Home
- Community
- Spiritual connection

Now, for each area you circled, write one honest sentence about the *energy* you've been broadcasting. Not the story you wish were true. Not what you post, affirm, or hope for. The felt state you return to most days.

For example:

- "In money, I oscillate between trust and panic."
- "In love, I want closeness, but I brace for abandonment."
- "In health, I'm exhausted and hard on myself."
- "In purpose, I feel called but afraid to be seen."

This isn't a diagnosis. It's a snapshot. Awareness is power because you cannot change a pattern you refuse to name. And the moment you name it, the system is already beginning to shift.

A Story of the Quiet Shift

One woman named Sarah told me she almost quit on Day 5.

Nothing external had changed. There were no signs she could point to. No dramatic breakthroughs. No visible movement in the thing she was manifesting. What *had* changed was how she felt inside, and she didn't like it. She felt bored. Restless. Slightly irritated. The novelty had worn off, and impatience was creeping in. Her mind started whispering familiar thoughts: *This isn't working. I should be further along by now. Maybe this just isn't for me.*

Normally, that's where she would stop. That uncomfortable, neutral space had always been her exit point. But this time, she stayed. Not because she felt inspired, but because she had committed to the structure. She kept doing the practices. She kept checking in. She didn't force optimism. She just didn't abandon herself.

About a week later, something subtle caught her attention. She realized she was responding differently to stress. When her kids were loud or demanding, she wasn't snapping. When emails piled up, she wasn't avoiding her inbox. She felt steadier, more grounded, less reactive. Life hadn't gotten easier, but *she* had become more regulated.

Three weeks later, an opportunity appeared that mirrored exactly what she had been working toward. It felt almost obvious when it arrived. Looking back, she said to me, "I didn't realize the work was already done before the thing showed up."

That's how this works. The external result is often the last thing to change. The real shift happens quietly first. And if you stay through that quiet phase, reality catches up.

The Blueprint Is Forgiving

You will miss days. That's part of being human, not a flaw in the process. You will forget rituals, rush through a morning, or fall asleep without doing your evening integration. You will have moments where old patterns resurface and it feels like you've slipped backward. None of this undoes the work you've already done. This is not a fragile system that collapses the moment you're imperfect. It is designed to be resilient, just like your nervous system is meant to be.

What matters is not uninterrupted consistency but return. Every time you come back to the practice, you strengthen the neural pathway you're building. Every moment of repair teaches your body that alignment is something you can return to, not something you can lose. Every reset reinforces identity. You are not starting over. You are continuing, with more awareness than before.

Making This Blueprint Your Own

As you move forward, this blueprint becomes increasingly personal. Your affirmations will evolve as your desires clarify and your sense of safety expands. Your check-ins will deepen, becoming less about monitoring and more about listening. Inspired actions will feel more intuitive, less effortful, and more aligned with who you are becoming.

Over time, integration becomes second nature. You don't have to remember to align, you simply do. The structure stays, steady and supportive, while your expression grows.

Closing: Living the Blueprint

By now, one thing should be clear: you don't need more tools.

What you need is integration. You need a way of living that doesn't fall apart when life gets busy, emotions fluctuate, or certainty disappears.

That is what the 24/7 Manifestation Blueprint offers.

This blueprint is not about control. It's not about managing every thought, forcing yourself into positivity, or performing alignment so the universe responds. It's about relationship. A relationship with your energy. With your nervous system. With the version of you that already knows where you're going, even when the path isn't fully visible yet.

When manifestation becomes relational instead of transactional, everything changes. You stop asking, *"What do I need to do to get this?"* and start asking, *"How do I stay aligned with who I'm becoming?"* The focus shifts from outcomes to coherence. From force to familiarity. From effort to rhythm.

This blueprint works because it meets you where real change happens: inside ordinary days. Inside mornings when you're groggy, afternoons when something triggers you, evenings when you're tempted to check out instead of check in. It doesn't require perfection. It only requires return. Every time you come back to alignment, even gently, you strengthen the pathway. Every repair builds trust. Every repetition reinforces identity.

You are not learning how to manifest something outside of yourself. You are learning how to live in a way that makes manifestation inevitable. When alignment becomes your baseline, your choices become clearer. Your actions become more grounded. Your energy becomes more coherent. And reality begins responding not as a reward, but as a reflection.

This blueprint is not about becoming someone else. It's about becoming congruent with who you are already becoming, letting your brain, body, and energy field move together instead of pulling against each other. When that happens, life stops feeling like something you're trying to manage and starts feeling like something you're participating in.

In the next chapter, we'll deepen this work by breaking down the Four Pillars of Manifestation Mastery. You'll see exactly how mindset, emotion, identity, and action interact inside this blueprint, and how to strengthen each one without overwhelm. The Four Pillars are what create your reality. The Anchors are how you stabilize them in your daily life.

Keep practicing. Keep returning. Let alignment become something you live, not something you visit. Because once you live it, your life responds.

Reflection Questions

1. Which part of the blueprint feels most supportive right now?
2. Which part feels resistant?
3. What would consistency look like for you, realistically?

There is no right answer.
Only honesty.

CHAPTER 5

The Four Pillars of Manifestation Mastery

If you have ever said, "I know what I want … so why am I not getting it?"

Welcome. You are exactly where you're supposed to be because wanting is not the problem.

Most of us do not struggle with desire. We struggle with inconsistency. Not the kind you can fix with a planner, a vision board, or a more aesthetic morning routine. I mean the deeper kind. The kind where your mouth says, "I'm ready," and your body says, "Absolutely not." The kind where your mind is dreaming and your nervous system is bracing. The kind where you can see the life you want so clearly, but you cannot hold the frequency long enough to meet it.

This chapter is here to change that.

This chapter will not give you another list of techniques to try for three days and abandon on Day 4. It won't tell you to "just think positive" when your reality is loud. This chapter will give you a framework that makes manifestation make sense, not just spiritually, but practically. Not just conceptually, but in your actual life with your actual patterns, triggers, bills, relationships, history, habits, hopes, and hangups.

The Four Pillars are the foundation of the 24/7 Manifestation Method because they create one thing the universe responds to every single time: **coherence**.

As discussed in Chapter 3, coherence is when what you think, what you feel, who you believe you are, and what you do are aligned. It's when you're no longer sending mixed signals. The message you're broadcasting is clean and consistent.

When one pillar conflicts with the others, you get mixed results, even when you're doing "everything right." You can have big inspiration followed by a quiet collapse. You can take action and still feel stuck. You can say the affirmations while your body is tense. You can "believe" in your dream and still sabotage the moment it gets close.

That is not because you are broken. It's because one or more pillars are sending a different message than the rest of you.

So instead of giving you another method to perform, I'm giving you a diagnostic tool. A way to locate the distortion in your signal and repair it, quickly. Something you can use for the rest of your life, no matter what you are manifesting.

The Four Pillars are

- mindset,
- emotion,
- identity, and
- aligned action.

Think of them as the four channels of your manifestation signal. If one channel is distorted, the entire broadcast gets fuzzy. If all four channels agree, your signal becomes clean, clear, and magnetic.

Pillar 1: Mindset

Mindset is where most people naturally start. And that makes sense. Your thoughts are powerful. Your beliefs shape perception. What you focus on determines what your brain highlights and what it filters out. But I want to be very clear about something right away.

Mindset is necessary, but mindset alone is not enough.

THOUGHTS ARE SEEDS, NOT GUARANTEES

If you plant a seed in dry soil, it does not matter how much you believe in the seed. It will not grow. No amount of positive thinking can override an environment that is not ready to support what you are planting.

Manifestation is not about belief alone. It is about consistent inner conditions.

So, what is mindset, really?

Mindset is the repeated mental narrative you live inside of. It is what you assume is true about yourself, your worth, what is safe, what is possible, how life works, how relationships work, and how money works. These assumptions are not always conscious. In fact, the most powerful ones usually aren't.

If your mindset says, "People always leave," your nervous system scans for abandonment. You interpret neutral moments as rejection. You hold back. You test people. You brace. And eventually, you call this intuition, even though it is conditioning.

If your mindset says, "I'm behind," your system lives in urgency. You rush. You overcommit. You feel anxious even when you are doing fine. You burn out. Then you use the burnout as proof that you really are behind.

If your mindset says, "I can handle this," your body stays more open. Your breath is steadier. Your choices are cleaner. You solve problems faster because you are not panicking while solving them.

Your thoughts are not just thoughts. They are instructions your nervous system follows.

THE MOST COMMON MINDSET MISTAKE

The most common mindset mistake is forcing thoughts your body does not believe.

You say, "I am abundant," while your stomach tightens.

You say, "Everything is working out," while your chest constricts.

You say, "I am confident," while your shoulders creep toward your ears.

That is not mindset mastery. That is strain.

Your subconscious does not learn from words alone. It learns from the combination of language, emotional imprint, and bodily response. The body always votes, and it votes faster than the mind.

So, in the 24/7 Manifestation Method, mindset work is not about lying to yourself or overriding discomfort. It is about choosing thoughts that are expansive and believable enough to land safely in your system.

Instead of "I'm a millionaire," you might start with something true:

- "I am building my capacity to receive."
- "I am learning to trust myself with money."
- "It is safe for me to have more support than I'm used to."
- "I am becoming a woman who follows through."

These thoughts are not smaller. They are smarter.

Because your subconscious cannot integrate what you do not feel safe embodying.

MINDSET MASTERY: YOU STOP BELIEVING EVERY THOUGHT

Mindset mastery is not about controlling every thought that passes through your mind. That would be exhausting, unrealistic, and unnecessary. The human mind produces thousands of thoughts a day, many of them recycled, reactive, or rooted in old conditioning. Mastery does not mean silence. It means discernment.

Mindset mastery begins the moment you stop treating every thought like a fact.

Instead of being automatically pulled into the story your mind offers, you learn to pause and question it. You create just enough space to ask:

Is this thought true?

Is it useful?

Is it aligned with the life I am building?

Is this my wisdom speaking, or my conditioning repeating itself?

That pause is powerful. It breaks the spell. When you question a thought, you are no longer inside it. You are observing it. And observation restores choice.

This is where people often feel immediate relief. Not because the thoughts disappear, but because they no longer have authority. You stop being hypnotized by your own inner dialogue. You move from being managed by your mind to being in relationship with it. You become the observer, not the servant.

PRACTICE: THE THOUGHT AUDIT

For the next 24 hours, gently notice the three thoughts you repeat most often. Not the thoughts you post, affirm, or wish you believed. The ones you actually live inside of.

Write them down.

Then ask:

If I believed this thought for a year, what result would it create?

What emotional state does it reinforce?

What behaviors does it lead me toward or away from?

Patterns will emerge quickly. And once you can see a pattern clearly, it begins to loosen its grip.

Mindset is the doorway. It opens possibility.

Now let's talk about what actually makes that possibility magnetic.

Pillar 2: Emotion

Emotion is one of the most honest indicators of what you are broadcasting into the world. Not because emotions are dramatic, but because they are precise. Emotions are not just internal experiences. They are signals. They shape your posture, your tone of voice, the boundaries you set, the risks you take, the patience you have, and the resilience you can access when things don't move immediately.

YOUR FREQUENCY HAS A FEELING

Emotions directly influence your nervous system. And your nervous system, in turn, influences your behavior. This is why two people can hold the same mindset language and still experience completely different outcomes. One person can say, "I am supported," and feel a sense of warmth, openness, and ease in their body. Another person can say the same words and feel tightness, suspicion, or the urge to stay guarded. Same sentence. Entirely different signal.

Manifestation doesn't respond to the words.

It responds to the frequency underneath them.

EMOTIONAL MASTERY IS NOT "BEING POSITIVE"

Emotional mastery does not mean being happy all the time. It does not mean bypassing sadness, fear, anger, or grief. It means you can feel an emotion without letting it define who you are or dictate how you move. You can experience fear without letting fear run your decisions. You can feel sadness without collapsing into hopelessness. You can feel anger and use it as information and clarity instead of turning it into self-attack or outward harm.

Emotions are energy in motion. They are meant to move through you, not get stuck inside you.

What blocks manifestation is not "negative emotion." What blocks manifestation is unprocessed emotion that loops. When emotion doesn't move, it becomes a pattern. Patterns solidify into identity. Identity shapes action. And action creates results. This is why emotional work is not optional. It is foundational.

THE EMOTIONAL LOOP THAT CREATES DELAYS

There is a loop I see again and again.

You decide you want something.

You feel inspired.

Then fear appears.

Your body tightens.

You start overthinking.

You hesitate.

You stall.

Then shame shows up for stalling.

So, you avoid the desire to avoid the shame.

And eventually you conclude, "Maybe it's not meant for me."

That is not intuition.

That is dysregulation.

When your nervous system learns to associate desire with danger, it will shut down momentum every time. Not because you are weak. Not because you lack discipline. But because your system is doing exactly what it was trained to do: protect you.

Emotional mastery teaches your body that desire is not a threat. And when desire feels safe, movement becomes possible again.

EMOTIONAL REGULATION IS A MANIFESTATION SKILL

Emotional regulation is not a side skill to manifestation. It *is* the skill. When you learn how to regulate your internal state, you become someone who can hold expansion without imploding. You can feel excitement without tipping into panic. You can sit inside uncertainty without immediately spiraling into worst-case scenarios. You can experience disappointment without collapsing into self-doubt or shutting down your desires. You can stay in trust even while life is rearranging itself behind the scenes. And perhaps most importantly, you can keep moving forward even when the timeline isn't immediate and there's no external proof yet.

That is manifestation mastery.

Not a perfect mood.

A resilient system.

A regulated nervous system allows you to remain available for what you're calling in. It keeps your signal steady instead of reactive. Instead of swinging between hope and despair, you develop the capacity to stay present, grounded, and responsive.

PRACTICE: THE 90-SECOND RESET

When a strong emotion arises, your body can naturally process it in about 90 seconds *if you don't feed it with story*. The practice is simple, but powerful:

Name the feeling. "This is fear." "This is shame." "This is anger."

Breathe slowly and deeply.

Notice where the sensation lives in your body.

Let the sensation rise and fall without trying to fix it.

Then choose the next aligned response.

This is how you interrupt emotional loops that keep your frequency stuck. You stop rehearsing the old track. And you start choosing a new one.

Pillar 3: Identity

Identity is the engine of manifestation.

Mindset gives you ideas.

Emotion gives you frequency.

Identity gives you permission.

Identity is who you believe you are at your core and what feels *normal* for you. It's the version of you that your subconscious recognizes as "me." And because the subconscious is designed to preserve consistency, it will always guide you back to what feels familiar, even if what's familiar no longer serves you.

WHO YOU BELIEVE YOU ARE DETERMINES WHAT YOU RECEIVE

Identity determines what you expect, what you tolerate, what you reach for, and what you subconsciously reject. It shapes what feels possible and, just as importantly, what feels *allowed*.

This is why so many people do mindset work and emotional work and still feel stuck. They are trying to manifest a life their identity doesn't yet have permission to hold.

You can want abundance, but if your identity is "I'm the one who struggles," your nervous system will return you to struggle because it feels known.

You can want love, but if your identity is "I'm too much," you will shrink when closeness arrives.

You can want visibility, but if your identity is "I'm safer when I'm unnoticed," you will procrastinate every opportunity that requires being seen.

This isn't self-sabotage.

It's loyalty.

Identity is loyal to the version of you that kept you safe.

IDENTITY IS A SET OF RULES

Every identity carries rules, most of which were never chosen consciously. They were formed through survival, family dynamics, culture, and moments where you learned what worked and what didn't.

If your identity is "I'm the responsible one," your rules might sound like this:

- Rest is lazy.
- Support is risky.
- Control equals safety.
- Emotions are inconvenient.

If your identity is "I'm the strong one," your rules might sound like this:

- Asking for help is weakness.
- Vulnerability is dangerous.
- Softness has a cost.
- I have to carry everything.

If your identity is "I'm the nice one," you might sound like this:

- Boundaries are rude.
- Honesty creates conflict.
- Saying no makes me unlovable.
- My needs come last.

Identity is powerful because it's invisible. It feels like truth. It feels like personality. It feels like *you*. But many identities were built in survival seasons. They were strategies, not destinies. And strategies can be updated.

When identity shifts, reality follows.

IDENTITY PROTECTS CONSISTENCY

Your subconscious prefers consistency over happiness.

Not because it wants you to suffer, but because consistency feels safe. It feels predictable. It feels controllable. And to a nervous system, control often equals survival.

So, when you decide to change your life, your identity may push back. Not because it hates your dream. Not because you're doing something wrong. But because your system is asking a very practical question: *Is this still safe to be?*

This is why you can feel deeply inspired, take a few aligned steps, and then suddenly feel tired, distracted, doubtful, or strangely indifferent. One moment you're excited. The next you're "over it." That swing can feel confusing, even discouraging.

But that's not failure.

That's identity preserving itself.

Your system is saying:

"We don't do that."

"That's not who we are."

"This is unfamiliar, so it might be dangerous."

This is the moment many people label themselves as self-sabotaging. But most self-sabotage isn't self-hatred. It's self-protection running on outdated rules. Your identity is trying to keep you consistent with what it knows, even if what it knows was built in a very different chapter of your life.

IDENTITY SHIFTS THROUGH EVIDENCE

Identity does not change through wishing or affirming alone.

Identity changes through evidence.

Evidence comes from behavior.

Behavior comes from choices.

And choices come from what your nervous system believes is safe.

That's why identity shifting is not pretending. It's preparing.

You become the person who follows through by following through.

You become the person who is supported by practicing receiving support.

You become the person who is respected by respecting yourself.

You become the person who is visible by allowing yourself to be seen.

You don't wait to feel ready. You train readiness through small, repeated acts of alignment.

And this is where we go deeper.

Because identity doesn't shift all at once. It shifts at the exact point where familiarity breaks and a new pattern begins to form.

IDENTITY IS NOT A VIBE; IT'S A PATTERN

Now let's bring it back to something very practical.

Identity is not what you say you want.

It's not your vision board.

It's not your intentions.

Identity is what you repeatedly do, choose, tolerate, and avoid, especially when you're tired, stressed, or emotionally activated. It's the pattern your system returns to when no one is watching and nothing is scripted.

That's why the fastest way to see your identity is to look at your defaults:

What do you do when you feel overwhelmed?

What do you do when you feel rejected?

What do you do when you feel uncertain?

What do you do when you feel excited or hopeful?

Those moments reveal who you believe you are and what feels normal to you.

If you want peace but you chronically overcommit, your identity might be, "I am only worthy when I prove myself."

If you want abundance but you undercharge, overgive, or avoid looking at your finances, your identity might be, "It's not safe for me to receive."

If you want love but consistently choose emotionally unavailable people, your identity might be, "Love must be earned."

These are not flaws.

They are not accusations.

They are data points.

And data gives you power, because once you can see the pattern, you can begin to choose differently.

THE ROLE OF SAFETY IN IDENTITY

Your nervous system will not let you sustain a new identity if it does not feel safe. If the identity you desire is visible, wealthy, loved, supported, powerful, or peaceful, your body must learn that those states are not a threat. Otherwise, you will unconsciously return to the old identity simply because it feels familiar. This is why identity work is never just mental. It is emotional and somatic. Real change happens when your system learns it is safe to expand.

Pillar 4: Aligned Action

This is the pillar where some spiritual people get uncomfortable.

Because part of us wants manifestation to be all energy and no effort.

The download without the discipline.

The miracle without the movement.

The blessing without the bravery.

I get it. Truly.

But aligned action is not optional.

THE UNIVERSE LOVES MOVEMENT

Action is part of the signal.

Action is how you communicate commitment to your subconscious.

Action is how you generate evidence.

Action is how you meet your future in real time.

The universe responds to movement.

Not frantic movement.

Not hustle that burns your nervous system to the ground.

Aligned movement.

WHAT ALIGNED ACTION ACTUALLY MEANS

Aligned action means your actions match your intention and your capacity.

If you want peace, aligned action includes boundaries, rest, and simplification.

If you want abundance, aligned action includes tracking your money, charging with integrity, making decisions that honor your value, and expanding your ability to receive.

If you want love, aligned action includes emotional availability, choosing people who can meet you, communicating your needs, and releasing patterns that keep you guarded.

Aligned action is not punishment.

It is embodiment.

It is you acting like the person who believes it is possible, even before proof arrives.

Most people don't avoid action because they're lazy.

They avoid action because action represents risk.

Action means exposure.

It means change.

It means stepping out of the familiar identity.

So, the subconscious offers reasonable-sounding delays:

"Let me think about it more."

"I need more information."

"I'll do it when I feel ready."

"I should perfect this first."

That's not intuition.

That's fear wearing a cardigan.

Aligned action is often simple.

It's not always comfortable.

But it is clean, steady, and identity-shifting.

Putting the Four Pillars Together: Coherence Is the Magic

Now we bring it all together.

If something isn't manifesting, this is not the moment to panic, self-diagnose, or assume you're doing something wrong. This is the moment to get curious. Manifestation is not a mystery. It's a system. And systems can be audited.

When results feel inconsistent, the answer is almost always coherence.

Use this simple Coherence Check:

Mindset: What am I repeatedly thinking?

Emotion: What am I repeatedly feeling?

Identity: Who am I repeatedly being?

Action: What am I repeatedly doing or avoiding?

You're not looking for perfection. You're looking for alignment.

If one pillar is broadcasting a different message than the others, the signal becomes mixed. And mixed signals create mixed results: Inspiration followed by collapse. Progress followed by retreat. Wanting followed by frustration.

Let's make this real.

EXAMPLE: MONEY

Desire: "I want more money."

Mindset says: "Money flows to me."

Emotion says: anxiety.

Identity says: "I'm not safe with money."

Action says: avoiding bank accounts, undercharging, overspending to soothe.

That's not failure. That's information. The pillars show you exactly where safety needs to be restored.

EXAMPLE: LOVE

Desire: "I want a healthy relationship."

Mindset says: "Love is possible."

Emotion says: guarded.

Identity says: "I'm safer alone."

Action says: choosing unavailable partners, testing instead of communicating, avoiding vulnerability.

Again, not failure. Information.

The pillars don't judge you. They guide you. When you repair the misaligned pillar, coherence returns. And when coherence returns, reality responds.

The Pillar Repair Method: What to Do When You're Triggered

This is one of the most important sections in this chapter because you can understand the pillars intellectually and still fall apart when you're triggered. That's normal. The goal isn't to never get activated. The goal is to know how to repair your signal quickly, without spiraling.

STEP 1: IDENTIFY THE TRIGGER

Name what happened. Not the whole story. Just the event.

"He didn't text back."

"My client asked for a refund."

"I saw someone else succeed."

"My bank account is lower than I want."

STEP 2: LOCATE THE PILLAR COLLAPSE

Ask: Where did I collapse first? Mindset, emotion, identity, or action? Usually, it's one primary pillar that falls, and the others follow.

STEP 3: REPAIR THE PILLAR, NOT THE CIRCUMSTANCE

This is the shift. Most people try to fix the circumstance while their inner world is spiraling, and that creates messy action. Repair the pillar first.

If it's **mindset**: Name the thought. Challenge it. Choose a truer thought.

If it's **emotion**: Regulate. Breathe. Let the sensation move without feeding the story.

If it's **identity**: Ask, "Who am I being right now?" and "Who do I choose to be instead?"

If it's **action**: Choose one clean step. One. Not ten.

STEP 4: RETURN TO COHERENCE

Coherence is not a mood. It's a decision you practice. This is how you stop giving your power away to triggers. You become the kind of woman who can hold herself. That is manifestation mastery.

Real-world Case Studies: How the Four Pillars Play Out in Real Life

Let's bring this into the real world because you don't need more theory. You need translation. The Four Pillars aren't abstract concepts. They show up clearly in everyday patterns, especially in the areas people care about most: money, love, and purpose. When something isn't manifesting, the pillars reveal why.

CASE STUDY 1: MANIFESTING MONEY

Desire: "I want consistent income."

On the surface, the mindset was there. She believed money was possible. But emotionally, money triggered anxiety, pressure, and shame, especially around spending or checking accounts. Her identity quietly said, "I'm not good with money. I always mess it up." So, her actions followed suit. She avoided budgeting, undercharged for her work, and overdelivered to compensate.

The repair wasn't more affirmations. It was identity. She began practicing the identity upgrade: "I am a woman who handles money with respect." Aligned actions followed. Weekly check-ins with her accounts. One intentional price increase. Tracking spending with compassion instead of judgment. As money felt safer to hold, it began to arrive more consistently.

CASE STUDY 2: MANIFESTING LOVE

Desire: "I want a healthy relationship."

Her mindset believed love existed, but emotionally she stayed guarded and hypervigilant. Her identity said, "I'm safer alone" and "I have to earn love." Her actions reflected that. She chose emotionally unavailable partners, tested instead of communicated, and avoided vulnerability.

The repair focused on emotional regulation and identity rehearsal. Safety came first. Then aligned action. Honest communication. Releasing half-effort connections. The signal changed, and so did who she attracted.

CASE STUDY 3: MANIFESTING PURPOSE

Desire: "I want to live my purpose."

She believed she was meant for more, but fear and overwhelm dominated. Her identity whispered, "I'm not ready. I'm not qualified." Action stalled through perfectionism and procrastination. The repair was identity plus action. One small visibility step daily. Evidence accumulated. Identity shifted. Purpose became real.

A Seven-day Pillar Training: The Four Pillars as a Lifestyle

If you want this chapter to become lived wisdom instead of something you simply understand, commit to this seven-day training. Think of it as a gentle reset that helps your system integrate the Four Pillars in real time, through experience rather than effort.

DAY 1: MINDSET

Write your desire clearly. Then answer: *"What do I currently believe about this?"* Choose one belief to question or soften.

DAY 2: EMOTION

Notice your dominant emotional state throughout the day. Ask: *"What emotion do I need to practice to become a match?"* Practice regulation three times.

DAY 3: IDENTITY

Write: *"The old identity says . . . "* and *"The new identity says . . . "* Then take one action the old identity would avoid.

DAY 4: ALIGNED ACTION

Ask: "What is one clean step I can take today?" Do it before noon.

DAY 5: COHERENCE

Audit all Four Pillars on one page. Notice congruence and conflict. Choose one repair.

DAY 6: RECEIVING

Practice receiving one thing without deflecting. Let it land.

DAY 7: INTEGRATION

Reflect on what changed *in you*. Because you are the signal.

Closing: This Is What Mastery Looks Like

Manifestation mastery is not about getting everything you want instantly or bending reality to your will. It is about becoming the kind of woman who can *hold* what she asks for without collapsing, sabotaging, or shrinking when it arrives. Plenty of people can manifest a moment, a breakthrough, or a short-lived win. Far fewer can manifest a life that feels stable, expansive, and sustainable.

A life requires coherence. It requires emotional capacity, so you can stay present when things grow bigger than what you're used to. It requires identity leadership, so you are no longer led by old patterns when discomfort arises. And it requires action that actually matches your desire, not just your intentions.

This is why the 24/7 Manifestation Method works. It is not a ritual you perform when you're inspired or a tool you reach for when something feels wrong. It is a way of living that trains your nervous system, identity, and energy to move together. You stop manifesting in bursts. You start manifesting consistently.

And once you learn how to work the pillars, you stop feeling at the mercy of your moods, your past, your fear, or your conditioning. You become the creator again. Not because you forced the universe, but because you finally became a match for what you're calling in.

Reflection Questions

1. Which pillar is strongest for you right now?
2. Which pillar feels most inconsistent?
3. Where do you feel the biggest gap between what you want and who you are being?
4. What emotion is most dominant in your daily life lately?
5. What is one belief you are willing to question this week?

CHAPTER 6

Rewiring Your Habits and Daily Life

In Chapters 4 and 5, the framework for the blueprint was created. This chapter is where you actually move in and start living there. This is where things become personalized and actionable.

You don't need another idea. You need a new normal.

The hardest part of change isn't knowing what to do. It's waking up on a random Tuesday and doing it when no one is watching—when you're tired, when you're irritated.

When the old version of you feels easier.

You can have the clearest vision in the world. You can journal it, visualize it, speak it out loud, cry over it under a full moon, and still wake up the next morning and reach for the same patterns you've always reached for.

Not because you don't want your dream badly enough. Not because you're lazy. Not because you're doing it wrong. But because your nervous system and your subconscious mind are loyal to what feels familiar.

That loyalty is what we call a habit.

A habit is simply your brain conserving energy by repeating what it already knows. It prefers familiar over expansive. It runs on efficiency, not inspiration, which is why manifestation does not become your lifestyle through one breakthrough moment or through one powerful workshop or one inspired journaling session where you felt aligned for three hours and then found yourself bracing again by Tuesday morning.

Transformation happens when the practice becomes normal.

When alignment is not a mood, but a rhythm.

When the way you think, feel, decide, speak, and act is coherent on an ordinary weekday, not just during a spiritual high.

Rewiring your habits is not about becoming rigid. It's not about turning yourself into a productivity machine or building routines so strict that you feel like you've failed by noon.

It's about designing a daily life that supports the version of you who already has what you desire. Manifestation is not a one-time event. It is an identity you practice. And the identity you practice repeatedly is the reality you eventually live.

Most people treat habits like a discipline problem.

They think, "If I were more motivated, I'd do it."

"If I were more consistent, I'd follow through."

"If I really wanted it, I wouldn't procrastinate."

That is not how habit change works. Motivation is unreliable. It's a mood. Habits are not built by mood. They're built by repetition.

And repetition becomes automatic through one thing: **association**.

Your brain links actions to emotional outcomes.

If your brain links "working out" to shame, you will resist it.

If your brain links "checking your bank account" to panic, you will avoid it.

If your brain links "being visible" to rejection, you will procrastinate.

If your brain links "rest" to guilt, you will sabotage it.

You can want the habit, but if your nervous system believes the habit is unsafe, you will drift back to the old pattern.

So, the question is not: "How do I force myself to change?"

The question is: "How do I make the new habit feel safe enough to repeat?"

That is rewiring.

Rewiring Is Not Just Behavior, It's Identity

A few years ago, I watched someone in one of my programs do something so small it almost looked like nothing. She kept saying she wanted a calmer life. More peace. More space. But every morning, the first thing she did in her New York City apartment was hit snooze … then grab her phone ... then start her day already behind as a caffeine tracking zombie.

When we talked about it, she said, "I just need more discipline."

No. What she needed was a new identity. Because a habit is not just something you do. It's a quiet vote for who you believe you are. Hitting snooze is not just extra sleep. It's practicing the identity of someone who avoids discomfort. Overcommitting is not just being busy. It's rehearsing the belief that your needs do not matter. Checking your phone before you breathe is not just scrolling. It's living like regulation comes last.

This is not a moral judgment. It's a mirror. And the moment you can see the pattern without shame, you can change it with power. The fastest way to change a habit is not to fight the behavior. It's to upgrade the identity underneath it.

Habits are the daily language of identity, so in this chapter, we're going to implement the Four Pillars in real life with simple, repeatable practices that become your new normal.

A client once told me, "I've read all the books. I know what to do. I just can't seem to stick with it." She wasn't lacking knowledge. She was trying to change one layer of her life while the other two kept pulling her back. When you rewire a habit, you are not just changing behavior. You are changing three layers at once: your environment, your nervous system, and your identity.

- Layer one is your environment. Your environment is your silent teacher. It is always training you. If your bedroom is cluttered, your mind rarely rests. If your phone is your alarm clock, your day begins in reaction. If your calendar is overbooked, urgency becomes your baseline. Many people try to manifest peace inside a life that rehearses chaos. So, we adjust the space. Not perfectly. Intentionally.
- Layer two is your nervous system. You can write affirmations all day, but if your body feels unsafe, it will default to what it knows. Regulation is not about being calm all the time. It is about being steady enough to follow through.
- Layer three is identity. This is the deepest layer. Habits stick when they become who you are. Not "I'm trying," but "I am someone who."

And if you've been waiting to feel ready before acting, that waiting is simply a well-practiced habit. And habits can be rewired.

YOUR SUBCONSCIOUS LOVES PATTERNS MORE THAN GOALS

I've never met a woman who didn't have goals. She wants love. She wants financial freedom. She wants confidence. She wants peace. Her vision board is clear. Her journal is full. Her intentions are sincere. And yet, nothing shifts.

Not because the goal is wrong, but because your subconscious does not organize around goals. It organizes around what feels normal. Your conscious mind loves the idea of someday. Your subconscious is loyal to today.

It pays attention to what you repeat. It tracks what your body expects. It memorizes your emotional baseline. And whatever you rehearse becomes your default.

This is why the 24/7 Manifestation Method is not just about what you write in the morning and at night. The journal matters. The affirmation matters. But what transforms your life is what happens in between.

Because the in-between is where your identity is revealed.

Your reality is shaped in micro-decisions: In the breath you take instead of reacting. In the boundary you hold when it would be easier to collapse. In the way you speak to yourself after you make a mistake. In the moment you act before you feel fully ready.

That is your signal. So, if you want a different reality, you do not just need a bigger goal. You need a different default. And defaults are not declared. They are practiced.

The Habit Loop You're Living In

A client once told me, "I don't know why I keep doing this. I know better." But knowing better and doing differently are not the same thing. Habits don't run on logic. They run on loops. Every habit follows a simple pattern: cue, behavior, reward.

Something triggers you. You respond. You get a payoff. The payoff is everything.

We don't repeat habits because they're good for us. We repeat them because they reward us. Sometimes the reward is obvious. Sugar tastes good. Sometimes it's subtle. Avoiding conflict feels safer than speaking up. Sometimes it's emotional. Scrolling numbs discomfort. Overworking prevents you from feeling inadequate. Staying busy keeps you from sitting with yourself.

Take overthinking. The cue is uncertainty. The behavior is analyzing, researching, delaying. The reward is temporary relief from the fear of being wrong. Overthinking is not your personality. It's protection, which means the solution is not to shame yourself into stopping.

The solution is to create a new response to uncertainty that still gives you safety but also moves you forward. Because if you want to change the habit, you don't just remove the behavior. You redesign the reward. And that's where rewiring begins.

You repeat what you hate because it feels familiar. Your nervous system would rather repeat a familiar pain than risk an unfamiliar freedom. And familiar feels safe, even when it hurts.

Your nervous system is not designed to chase happiness. It is designed to seek predictability. It wants what it recognizes. So, if you were raised in chaos, calm can feel unsettling. If you were raised in criticism, kindness can feel suspicious. If love was inconsistent, stability can feel almost boring. If money was scarce, abundance can feel dangerous.

So, you recreate what your body knows. Not because you enjoy suffering but because your system understands it. This is why habit change is deeper than willpower. It is nervous system work. It is identity work. It is teaching your body that a new pattern is safe enough to live in.

That is the real work.

The 24/7 Manifestation Method as Habit Rewiring

The 24/7 Manifestation Method was never just about positive thinking. It was designed for rewiring. It works with two of the most impressionable windows of your day: the moments right after you wake up and right before you fall asleep. In those spaces, your brain naturally shifts states. Your critical mind softens. Your subconscious becomes more receptive.

So, when you repeat an affirmation and pair it with emotion during those windows, you are not just "manifesting." You are rehearsing a new identity. You are installing a new pattern. You are teaching your nervous system what is safe, possible, and normal.

And what you rehearse consistently becomes real. But here is the key: the writing alone is not enough. You can imprint the morning and close the night beautifully and still contradict yourself all afternoon.

This chapter is about the in-between. Because that is where identity stops being imagined and starts being lived.

Why Action Is the Cure for Fear

There is a moment almost everyone misinterprets. You feel the pull toward something bigger: A new relationship. A new level of income. A bold post. A difficult conversation. A decision you have been circling for months. And just as you move toward it, fear shows up.

Most people read that fear as a stop sign. They assume discomfort means misalignment. They tell themselves, "If this were truly meant for me, it wouldn't feel this hard." But fear is not always a warning. Very often, it is a threshold.

Fear rises when you are about to outgrow your current identity: When you are about to be seen in a new way. When you are about to risk rejection, expansion, or change. When you are about to stop playing small in ways that once kept you safe.

So instead of asking, "How do I eliminate fear?" ask something more powerful: "What is this fear trying to protect?"

Fear protects the familiar. It protects the version of you that survived by staying quiet, staying agreeable, staying safe. At some point in your life, visibility may have led to criticism. Success may have led to pressure. Speaking up may have led to conflict. Your nervous system learned to hesitate for a reason.

But here is the shift. The cure for fear is not waiting for it to disappear. The cure is aligned action. Not reckless action. Not proving. Not hustling to override your body. Aligned action is movement that gently tells your nervous system, "We can do this. We can survive this. We are safe expanding." Courage is not something you wait to feel. It is something you build. You do not become fearless and then act. You act while afraid, and your brain updates its story.

Every time you take action and survive it, you create evidence. And evidence rewires identity. This is why affirmations alone can feel hollow. Your subconscious is not persuaded by your words. It is persuaded by your behavior. It wants proof. Action is proof. There is one rule that will change your life if you let it: never leave a decision without a commitment.

When you decide something but do not embody it, you create limbo. You decide you want change. Then you overthink. Then you wait for certainty. And momentum quietly dissolves. A decision becomes real the moment it becomes embodied.

The commitment does not need to be dramatic. It needs to be concrete. If you decide you want peace, set one boundary today. If you decide you want financial expansion, take one brave money action today. If you decide you want love, choose one self-respecting behavior today.

If you decide you want visibility, let yourself be seen once today.

Manifestation is not passive wishing. It is co-creation. And co-creation requires participation.

When you move, life moves. When you respond, reality reorganizes. Fear may walk beside you. That is human. Just don't let it drive.

The Habit That Makes Manifestation Inevitable

There is one habit that makes manifestation almost inevitable, and it is not journaling more, visualizing harder, or scripting longer. Those tools are powerful. But the habit that changes everything is simpler and deeper: you follow through on yourself.

When you say you are going to do something and you actually do it, your nervous system registers safety. It learns, "I can trust myself." And self-trust is magnetic. Self-trust changes how you walk into rooms, how you make decisions, how long you tolerate misalignment, and how quickly you recover when you wobble. And aligned actions compound. Follow-through is built the same way any habit is built: cue, behavior, reward. But here, the reward is not external. It is identity.

The reward is the quiet, powerful feeling of becoming someone who keeps promises to herself. And that changes everything.

The Follow-through Formula: A Daily Practice That Rewires You

For the next seven days, I want you to try something small and powerful. Each morning, before the day pulls you in a hundred directions, ask yourself: What is one thing future me would do today, even if I feel nervous?

Not ten things. One.

Choose something that stretches you slightly. A boundary. An email. A decision. A conversation. Then do it early, before overthinking has time to negotiate.

When you complete it, pause. Name it. "Look at me. I follow through." "I keep promises to myself." "I am becoming her."

This is not ego. It is conditioning. Your subconscious does not change because of good intentions. It changes because of repeated evidence. And evidence is built through action.

The Problem with Most Habit Advice

Most habit advice is built on an assumption that simply isn't true. It assumes you wake up regulated. It assumes you have endless emotional bandwidth. It assumes your life is already structured to support change.

So, you start strong: New routine. New rules. New motivation. And then life happens. You get tired. Triggered. Overwhelmed. Busy. Human. The problem isn't your discipline. It's the design.

Most people try to layer new habits on top of an environment and nervous system that are already stretched thin. So, the habit feels like effort instead of support. And effort, over time, burns out.

The 24/7 Manifestation Method doesn't ask: "How do I force consistency?" It asks: "How do I design my life so consistency becomes natural?"

And that answer lives in safety, structure, and rhythm.

Designing a Life That Makes Alignment Easier

Your habits are not just personal choices. They are environmental responses. You are not operating in a vacuum. You are operating inside a design. And that design is training you every single day.

Your phone trains urgency. Your calendar trains overwhelm. Your home trains your nervous system. Your conversations train your self-concept. Your schedule trains your priorities.

If you are trying to manifest peace inside a life that rehearses chaos, the problem is not your willpower. It is your design. Environment is a silent partner in your transformation. It either supports coherence or quietly sabotages it. There is no neutral.

If your phone is the first thing you touch in the morning, you are training your brain to look outward before you regulate inward. If your to-do list consistently exceeds your capacity, your nervous system learns that life equals threat. If your space is cluttered and unfinished, your body never fully drops into rest.

This is not about aesthetics. It is about signals. Your environment is constantly communicating to your subconscious what is normal, what is urgent, and what is safe. So, we adjust it. Not obsessively. Intentionally.

You do not need to overhaul your life. You need a few strategic shifts. First, protect the first ten minutes of your day. Those moments after waking are impressionable. Before your phone. Before other people's energy. Before urgency. Sit up. Breathe. Write your affirmation. Feel into who you are becoming. This is not discipline. It is imprint protection.

Second, reduce decision fatigue. Every unnecessary choice drains energy you could use for aligned action. Simplify where you can. Automate where possible. Preserve your willpower for what actually matters.

Third, create visual cues for identity. A journal on your nightstand whispers, "I reflect." Shoes by the door whisper, "I move." A cleared desk whispers, "I choose clarity."

Your environment should quietly reinforce who you are becoming. Design well, and alignment stops feeling like effort.

Habit Stacking: How Change Becomes Automatic

If you want change to last, you must make it easier than quitting. One of the most effective ways to do that is habit stacking. Habit stacking is simple: you attach a new behavior to something you already do. Your brain loves sequences. It thrives on rhythm. And you already have rhythms running all day long:

You brush your teeth.

You make coffee.

You unlock your phone.

You sit down at your desk.

You get into bed.

These are anchors. They are stable points in your day. So instead of adding something new and hoping you remember it, you stack it onto what already exists.

This is how the 24/7 Manifestation Method works in real life.

After waking → affirmation and identity cue.

Before sleep → affirmation and reflection.

After emotional activation → 90 seconds of regulation.

After a decision → a commitment.

After action → self-validation.

Suddenly, manifestation is not another task. It becomes a rhythm. Habit stacking works because it removes debate. And debate is where new habits collapse. When a practice rides an existing neural pathway, it stops feeling like effort and starts feeling automatic.

What to Do on the Days You Don't Feel Aligned

Let's talk about the days no one posts about. The tired days. The irritated days. The days your confidence dips, and your vision feels far away. The days you feel disconnected from everything you wrote in your journal. If your manifestation practice only works when you feel inspired, it's fragile. And fragile practices collapse under real life.

Alignment is not about staying "high vibe." It is not about pretending you feel expansive when you don't. Alignment is honesty plus regulation. It is choosing a conscious response instead of an unconscious reaction.

On low days, the practice does not disappear. It gets smaller. This is the Minimum Effective Dose rule. Not nothing. The minimum.

One affirmation instead of twenty-four.

One breath instead of a full meditation.

One aligned action instead of a dramatic leap.

One boundary instead of a confrontation.

The danger is not drifting. The danger is abandoning yourself when you drift. Manifestation mastery is not about perfection. It is about repair. You notice. You name it. You return. And every time you return without shame, you strengthen self-trust. And self-trust is magnetic.

The Emotional Habit That Changes Everything

There is one habit that quietly determines whether all the others stick. And it is not journaling.

It is not visualization. It is not even an action. It is self-validation.

Most people outsource their sense of safety. They wait for results, praise, recognition, proof, or approval before they allow themselves to feel secure. They tell themselves, "Once this works, then I'll relax. Once they notice, then I'll believe in myself."

But your nervous system cannot wait for the outcome to feel safe. It needs reassurance during the process.

So, we build validation in. Every time you take aligned action, you pause and acknowledge it. Not arrogantly. Intentionally.

"I did that."

"I followed through."

"I showed up."

"I didn't abandon myself."

At first, this can feel awkward. Your system may not be used to being seen by you. But over time, this habit builds internal safety, and internal safety reduces sabotage. When habits don't stick, ask a deeper question: What identity is this threatening?

If rest feels impossible, maybe productivity has become your identity.

If boundaries collapse, maybe being liked feels safer than being respected.

If visibility stalls, anonymity may feel protective.

The habit is rarely the real problem. The identity underneath it is negotiating. So instead of forcing yourself forward, soothe the part that feels unsafe. "We can survive this." "We are allowed to expand." "This is who we are becoming." That is how habits truly change.

A Daily Rhythm for Rewired Living

Let's bring this down to something you can actually live. Not something rigid. Reliable.

Morning: Imprint.

> An affirmation. An identity statement. One clear intention. You are setting the tone before the world sets it for you.

Midday: Regulation.

> A quick emotional check-in. One conscious breath. One reset. You return to yourself before drifting too far.

Evening: Integration.

An affirmation. One win. One moment of self-validation. You close the loop and reinforce who you are becoming.

That's it. Simple. Repeatable. Sustainable. And over time, powerful.

Why This Works When Other Things Don't

This approach works because it honors how you are actually wired. It respects your nervous system instead of fighting it. It respects identity instead of ignoring it. It respects your real life instead of pretending you live inside a motivational quote. It does not ask you to become someone else overnight. It asks you to practice becoming her.

And practice is how the brain rewires. Practice is how habits form. Practice is how manifestation stops feeling theoretical and starts feeling inevitable.

In the beginning, it will feel intentional. You will have to remember to pause. Remember to breathe. Remember to check your energy. Remember to choose differently. That phase is not weakness. It is training.

But that is not the destination. The destination is when you no longer have to remember, when you regulate before you spiral, when you speak up before resentment builds, and when you choose alignment before panic takes over.

That is not discipline. That is identity integration. Identity does not shift because you did something once. It shifts when you stop debating the choice. When the aligned response feels obvious, that is when your subconscious has learned.

MOMENTUM IS A NERVOUS SYSTEM STATE

Most people think momentum is about speed. Doing more. Moving faster. Pushing harder. It isn't. Momentum is safety in motion.

It exists when your nervous system trusts forward movement, when growth no longer feels like danger, when progress does not trigger collapse, and when expansion does not activate self-sabotage.

Real momentum feels almost effortless because your body is no longer fighting the direction you're going. You are not dragging yourself forward. You are allowing yourself to move forward.

That is why this chapter has focused on habits instead of hustle. Hustle forces movement. Momentum permits it.

And here is what quietly breaks momentum: not mistakes, but shame.

The moment you interpret discomfort as danger.

The moment you treat imperfection as failure.

The moment you abandon yourself for wobbling.

Momentum does not require perfection. It requires repair, the ability to pause, regulate, and return without self-punishment. And this is where we need to redefine failure.

FAILURE IS PART OF THE SYSTEM

Many people secretly believe, "If I were aligned, this wouldn't be hard." That belief is what actually stops momentum. Failure is not a detour from the path. It is part of the path.

Failure does not mean you are off track. It means you are expanding. It reveals which belief is still running, which habit needs strengthening, and where your nervous system still needs safety.

Failure is feedback. And feedback is how momentum becomes sustainable.

The universe does not respond to flawless execution. It responds to participation. The people who manifest expansive lives are not the ones who avoid failure. They are the ones who refuse to let failure remove them from motion.

They adjust.

They regulate.

They continue.

That is the creation loop:

Intention

Aligned action

Feedback

Regulation

Adjustment

Momentum

Then repeat. No collapse. No identity crisis. Just refinement. Momentum is not about never falling. It is about how quickly you return. And return is mastery.

When Old Patterns Resurface

There is something I want you to expect, not panic about: old patterns will resurface.

It's not because you are regressing, not because the work "didn't stick." It's because you are expanding. Growth does not delete conditioning overnight. It outgrows it gradually. And when you stretch into a new level of visibility, love, income, or leadership, the nervous system sometimes replays an old response.

An old fear.

An old urge.

An old coping strategy.

This is not failure. It is integration. The real question is not, "Why am I here again?" That question keeps you stuck in shame. The better question is, "How quickly can I return?" That is the measure of mastery. I teach what I call the 24-hour rule.

You are allowed to drift. You are allowed to wobble. You are allowed to have a day. But within 24 hours, you return. You regulate. You recommit. You take one aligned action. When you live this way, you stop turning moments into identities. You stop letting one choice define you.

You remain in leadership. And leadership builds trust in yourself.

Aligned Action as a Lifestyle

By this point, something subtle begins to shift. Aligned action is no longer dramatic. It is not a grand leap or a performative declaration. It becomes quiet. Integrated. Normal.

It looks like sending the email you used to avoid. Saying no without over-explaining. Resting without guilt. Choosing quality over urgency. Responding instead of reacting. Acting before you feel completely ready.

These are not flashy moves. They are identity moves. And identity moves compound.

Once your nervous system learns that aligned action is safe, it stops resisting it. You are no longer negotiating with fear for hours. You are no longer leaking energy through hesitation and self-doubt.

That is when manifestation begins to accelerate. Not because you are doing more. But because you are no longer fighting yourself while you do it.

The Habit of Self-leadership

At the highest level, what you are building here is not just better habits. You are building self-leadership.

Self-leadership means you no longer wait for motivation to move. You do not outsource decisions to other people's opinions. You do not abandon yourself when things feel uncomfortable. You stop negotiating endlessly with fear.

Instead, you guide yourself forward with clarity and compassion. And over time, that steadiness becomes your energetic signature. People feel it. Opportunities respond to it. Life reorganizes around it because leadership is coherence in motion.

The Daily Question That Changes Everything

If you took nothing else from this chapter, take this question: What would the version of me who trusts herself do next?

Not next month. Not when you feel more confident. Not when fear disappears. Next. That question cuts through the noise. It bypasses overthinking. It dissolves perfectionism. It interrupts the old fear narratives that keep you circling the same decision.

It places you back in leadership immediately. And motion is the language the universe understands. When you move, you shift. When you shift, reality reorganizes.

Eventually, the 24/7 Manifestation Method stops feeling like something you are "doing." It becomes how you relate to yourself. You notice when you drift. You regulate instead of spiraling. You act instead of waiting. You repair instead of punishing.

You stop trying to manifest and start responding. And life responds back. What people call "flow" is not accidental. It is trained. Built. Practiced. Day by day. Choice by choice.

A Long-term View of Your Life

Zoom out for a moment. You are not just manifesting a moment. You are building a life—a life that can hold love without panic. Money without guilt. Visibility without collapse. Peace without boredom. Success without self-betrayal.

That kind of life does not come from intensity. It comes from embodied defaults. Not rigid routines, but steady patterns. Habits that support you instead of draining you. Rhythms that make alignment normal instead of rare.

Defaults keep you moving even on imperfect days. That is what this chapter has been building. Not a temporary high. A sustainable life.

Practice: The Coherent Day

If you want to live this chapter instead of just understand it, simplify it. Each day, focus on three things:

One moment of regulation. Choose to calm your body instead of reacting. One aligned action. Take one step your future self would take, even if it feels uncomfortable.

One self-validation. Acknowledge yourself without waiting for external results. That's the work. Simple does not mean easy. It means repeatable. And repeatable becomes powerful.

Closing: You Are No Longer Waiting

As you close this chapter, I want you to understand something clearly:

You are not behind.

You are not late.

You are not broken.

You are learning how to live in coherence. And coherence changes everything. Your habits are no longer obstacles to overcome. They are the architecture of your future. Your daily life is no longer separate from your manifestation practice. It is the practice.

When your environment, nervous system, and identity begin working together, manifestation stops feeling like something you are trying to force. It becomes something that unfolds naturally. Not because the universe suddenly decided to reward you, but because you are no longer asking reality to shift while you remain the same.

You are moving.

You are participating.

You are becoming.

And life responds to that. Before you turn the page, pause. Place one hand on your chest and one on your belly. Take three slow breaths and say quietly:

"I am willing to practice alignment, even when it feels unfamiliar." That willingness is enough. You are not broken. You are patterned. And patterns can be changed.

Reflection Questions

Take your time with these.

1. Where in your life do you feel momentum building already?
2. Where do you still hesitate, and what identity is being protected there?
3. How do you typically respond to failure, and how would leadership respond instead?
4. What habit, if embodied consistently, would change your life the most?
5. What does aligned action look like for you right now, not in an ideal future?
6. Where are you ready to stop waiting and start participating?

Write honestly. This is not for perfection. This is for clarity.

PART III

Tips for Mastering the 24/7 Manifestation Method

CHAPTER 7

The Role of Surrender and Trust

There was a season in my life when I was doing everything right, and nothing was working.

I was aligned. I was consistent. I was devoted to my practices. I was regulating, journaling, taking action, following through. And still, doors stayed closed.

Not slammed. Not dramatically blocked. Just … unmoving. If you've ever been there, you know how disorienting that space can feel.

It's one thing when life isn't working and you know you're avoiding, numbing, or half-committing. It's another thing entirely when you're doing the work, honoring the process, embodying the identity, and reality seems to be taking its sweet time catching up.

That is where surrender and trust stop being pretty words and start becoming real work. This chapter is not about giving up.

It's about staying open without hardening.

It's about continuing to move without forcing.

It's about learning how to trust without disconnecting from your power.

Because surrender is one of the most misunderstood concepts in manifestation. And when it's misunderstood, it quietly derails everything.

The Moment Where Most People Break Trust

Most people don't stop trusting when things go wrong. They stop trusting when things go quiet, when there's no feedback. No confirmation. No visible progress. No obvious sign that the seeds are growing.

The signs slow down. The momentum plateaus. The excitement fades, and you're left alone with your commitment. That's when doubt creeps in.

Not the loud, dramatic kind. The subtle kind that whispers:

Maybe this isn't working. Maybe I misread the signs.

Maybe I should detach … but what if detaching means losing it?

This is the moment that separates people who manifest occasionally from people who build lives that respond to them. Because surrender is not something you practice at the beginning. Surrender is something you practice after you've already committed.

After you've taken action. After you've embodied the identity. After you've done what was yours to do. Surrender is what comes next.

Surrender Is Not the Same as Stopping

Let's clear something up immediately. Surrender is not passivity. Surrender is not resignation.

Surrender is not, "I guess it wasn't meant for me." Surrender is not spiritualized avoidance. Surrender is staying present without gripping the outcome. It is releasing the illusion that force creates flow.

And this matters because the nervous system cannot receive what the ego is strangling.

When you over-attach to a timeline, you create pressure. When you over-attach to an outcome, you create contraction. When you over-attach to control, you stop listening.

You stop noticing redirections. You stop sensing adjustments.

You stop responding to life in real time.

You become rigid. And rigidity blocks receptivity.

Surrender doesn't mean you stop choosing.

It means you stop micromanaging how life delivers.

It means you say: I will continue to show up. I will continue to act in alignment. And I release the demand that it must unfold in the exact way I imagined. That distinction changes everything.

Because when you release control without releasing commitment, your energy softens. Your breath deepens. Your posture shifts. Your nervous system loosens its brace.

And from that place, you can actually receive. Trust is not something you think your way into.

It is something your body learns. You learn it every time you survive uncertainty. Every time a delay turns out to be protection. Every time a redirection leads somewhere better. Every time you adapt without collapsing.

Trust is built through lived evidence, just like confidence, which means surrender is not weakness. It is nervous system maturity.

It is saying: I have done my part. Now I allow life to do its part. Not because I am powerless, but because I understand partnership.

Manifestation is not domination.

It is collaboration.

You embody the version of you who is ready. You take aligned action. You regulate your contradictions. You follow through. And then, at some point, you unclench. Not to quit. But to receive. That is the role of surrender. Not as the opposite of action. But as the refinement of it.

A Case Study About Control Disguised as Faith

Years ago, I watched a woman in one of my containers do everything "right."

She followed the practices.

She regulated her emotions.

She took aligned action.

She spoke her intentions clearly.

She embodied the identity.

On paper, she was the picture of coherence. But underneath it all, she was white-knuckling the outcome.

Every morning she scanned her life for proof.

Every delay felt personal.

Every redirection felt like rejection.

Every pause triggered panic.

She wasn't just manifesting. She was monitoring. Her nervous system was braced. Her energy was vigilant. She told me she trusted the process, but her body was in surveillance mode, waiting for confirmation that she wasn't about to be disappointed again.

One day, she said, "I think I need to surrender." But what she really meant was, "I don't want to feel let down anymore." That's not surrender. That's self-protection dressed up as spirituality.

True surrender would have sounded like this:

> "I am willing to keep showing up even if I don't understand the timing."
>
> "I trust myself enough to stay in motion without certainty."
>
> "I am not abandoning the desire. I am releasing the chokehold."

This is where surrender actually lives. Not in withdrawal. Not in pretending you don't care.

Not in numbing your hope so it can't hurt you.

But it is in grounded openness. It is continuing to move while loosening your grip. It is allowing life to respond in ways you did not script.

TRUST BEGINS WHERE CONTROL ENDS

Trust is not a personality trait. It is a relationship. And like any relationship, it is built through experience.

You do not trust life because someone told you to.

You trust life because you have survived not knowing before.

You have been redirected before.

You have lost things that made room for better ones.

You have grieved paths that were not yours.

You have been protected by delays you once resented.

Trust is retrospective before it is anticipatory. We trust backward first. And then, slowly, we learn to trust forward. There is a tension here that is not often discussed. When you are manifesting consciously, you are aware of your desires. And awareness intensifies attachment.

You are not just living your life. You are observing it. Tracking. Measuring. Interpreting.

Is this a sign? Is this a setback? Is this progress?

That hyper-awareness can quietly erode trust if you do not know how to regulate it. Because when you are watching too closely, you are rarely resting. This is why surrender must be learned after agency, not instead of it.

First, you act. First, you embody. First, you participate. Then you soften. Surrender without agency is avoidance. Agency without surrender becomes control. The 24/7 Manifestation Method teaches both.

THE DIFFERENCE BETWEEN SURRENDER AND COLLAPSE

There is a moment in every manifestation journey where effort stops working. Not because effort is wrong. But because the effort has done its job.

The soil is prepared. The seeds are planted. The patterns are shifting. The identity is upgrading. And now something else is required.

Presence. Patience. Receptivity.

This is where many people collapse instead of surrender. Collapse sounds like:

"I'm tired, so I'll stop caring."

"I don't want to hope anymore."

"I'll detach so it doesn't hurt."

"Maybe I never wanted it that much anyway."

Collapse is a shutdown. It pulls energy back. It numbs desire. It protects the ego from disappointment. Surrender sounds different:

"I am willing to rest without quitting."

"I can soften without giving up."

"I can pause without disconnecting."

"I can want this without strangling it."

Collapse contracts your energy. Surrender expands it. This is not semantics. Your nervous system knows the difference. In collapse, your body feels heavy, resigned, closed.

In surrender, your body feels open, steady, responsive. You are not chasing. You are not gripping. You are not shutting down.

You are available. And availability is magnetic. Manifestation is not about forcing outcomes; it is about becoming someone who can hold them. Surrender refines that capacity. It stabilizes your identity. It teaches your nervous system that uncertainty is not danger. And when your body stops bracing against what has not happened yet, you create space for what is meant for you to actually arrive. Surrender is not losing power. It is using power wisely. It is knowing when to push. And knowing when to open. That is mastery.

Trust Is a Nervous System Skill

We often think trust is mental. It's not. Trust lives in the body.

You can say you trust and still brace. You can affirm faith and still tighten. You can believe intellectually and still hold your breath.

The body tells the truth. When you truly trust, your system softens. Your breath deepens. Your jaw unclenches. Your posture shifts. Your reactions slow. And from that place, clarity emerges.

This is why trust cannot be forced. It must be felt. And feelings require safety. For years, I thought trust was something you declared, something you practiced like a mindset shift. Something you "chose." But what I've learned through thousands of conversations with women doing this work is this: trust is not a decision you make once. It is a nervous system capacity you build.

If your nervous system equates uncertainty with danger, you will grip. You will monitor. You will overanalyze. You will try to control outcomes so that you don't have to feel exposed. Not because you're weak but because you're wired to survive. The body does not understand "divine timing."

It understands safety. So, when something you deeply want feels delayed, the body doesn't interpret that as refinement. It interprets it as a threat. And that is why this chapter matters.

WHY THIS CHAPTER MATTERS NOW

By the time someone reaches Chapter 7, they have already done the visible work.

You've learned how to work with thoughts.

You've learned how to regulate emotion.

You've learned how to shift identity.

You've learned how to take aligned action.

You've learned how to rewire habits.

You are no longer passive. You are participating. Which means now comes the subtler work. Letting life meet you halfway. Not through waiting, but through listening. There is a moment when pushing harder creates resistance. And there is a moment when easing back allows momentum to return. Learning to tell the difference is mastery.

The 24/7 Manifestation Method gives you agency. It teaches you how to move. But without surrender, agency can turn into control. And control, when it becomes rigid, shuts down receptivity. Trust is what keeps power from becoming force. Trust is what allows agency to soften into wisdom.

A PERSONAL TURNING POINT

There was a decision I once wanted so badly that I stopped hearing myself. I convinced myself it was aligned. I convinced myself it was meant for me. I doubled down on my practices. I regulated. I journaled. I visualized. I took action. And every time something didn't move the way I expected, I felt it like a punch.

Every sign became a test.

Every delay became a threat.

Every alternate path felt like betrayal.

I told myself I was trusting. But my body was braced. I was vigilant, not surrendered. I was watching for confirmation, not listening for direction. And eventually, life did what life does when we're not listening. It interrupted me.

Not cruelly. Clearly.

The interruption wasn't dramatic. It was precise. A conversation shifted perspective. A door closed cleanly instead of cracking open. A realization that what I wanted was less important than who I was becoming. And in the quiet that followed, I realized something that changed how I work with manifestation forever:

Life was not withholding from me. It was trying to lead me. But I had been too busy directing. That was the moment trust deepened. Not as obedience. But as collaboration.

TRUST IS A DIALOGUE, NOT A DEMAND

When you truly trust, you stay curious.

You ask:

What is this showing me?

What am I being invited to release?

What is being rearranged for my benefit?

You don't rush to meaning. You don't dramatize the pause. You stay in relationship, and relationship requires listening. Listening means you are willing to not know immediately.

And not knowing can feel like danger to a nervous system trained on certainty. We live in a culture that equates speed with success and clarity with control. So, when things slow down, we assume something is wrong. But not knowing is where new timelines open.

If you already knew exactly how it would happen, you wouldn't be growing. Growth requires uncertainty. And uncertainty requires trust.

THE ROLE OF TIMING IN MANIFESTATION

Timing is not punishment. Timing is calibration.

There are versions of you that could not hold what you're calling in yet. Not because you're unworthy but because life is precise. If something arrived too early, it might overwhelm you.

If it arrived too late, you might resent it. If it arrived before you had stabilized your identity, you might sabotage it. Trust includes trusting timing:

Even when timing stretches your patience.

Even when it humbles your ego.

Even when it asks you to keep showing up without visible proof.

This is not weakness. It is strength refined.

Because anyone can be confident when results are immediate. It takes nervous system maturity to remain steady when they are not.

SURRENDER IS AN ACTIVE STATE

Surrender is not disengagement. Surrender is active receptivity. It is staying open while still moving. It is continuing to take aligned action while releasing the insistence that it must look a certain way. It is allowing detours without abandoning the destination.

Without agency, surrender becomes avoidance. With agency, surrender becomes wisdom.

You act. You regulate. You embody. You follow through. And then you soften your grip. Not to quit. To receive.

WHAT YOU'RE REALLY BEING ASKED TO TRUST

Ultimately, surrender is not about trusting the universe. It's about trusting yourself in the unknown, trusting that you can handle disappointment without collapsing; trusting that you can adapt if the plan changes; trusting that your worth is not dependent on outcomes; trusting that you will recognize the next step when it appears. That is what creates calm confidence.

Not blind faith. Grounded trust.

When your nervous system learns that uncertainty does not equal annihilation, something extraordinary happens. You stop panicking at pauses. You stop interpreting silence as rejection. You stop gripping timelines. You remain available. And availability is magnetic. Manifestation is not about forcing reality. It is about being stable enough to receive it.

A GENTLE REFRAME BEFORE WE GO ON

If you are in a season where things feel slower than you want, quieter than you expected, or different than you imagined, consider this:

What if nothing is wrong?

What if this is not a pause, but a recalibration?

What if life is not delaying you, but strengthening your capacity to receive?

Trust does not ask you to stop wanting. It asks you to stop gripping. And when the grip releases, movement often returns. Now we need to talk about the exact place where surrender gets misused: the moment when you call something "trust," but your nervous system has actually gone offline. We're going to look at how to trust the process without stalling, how to read obstacles correctly.

Life communicates when we don't listen the first time. Not to scare you, but to empower you. Once you understand how trust actually works, you stop confusing silence with failure.

Trusting the Process Without Stalling

Surrender does not mean you stop moving. It means you stop forcing. And those two things feel very different in the body. Forcing feels tight. Stalling feels heavy. Trust feels open and responsive.

Forcing is when your jaw clenches, your breath shortens, and you push because you're afraid nothing will happen if you don't. Stalling is when your shoulders drop, your energy collapses, and you tell yourself you're "letting go," but underneath, you've quietly stopped participating. Trust feels different.

Trust feels steady. Available. Willing. It feels like your feet are planted and your hands are open. The problem is that many people confuse surrender with inaction. They stop following through.

They stop initiating. They stop choosing. They stop risking.

And then they wait for life to move first. That is not trust. That is avoidance wearing spiritual language. True trust keeps you engaged.

Trust keeps you listening. It keeps you responsive instead of reactive. It keeps you moving without gripping. You still send the email. You still apply. You still have the conversation. You still take the step. You just stop demanding that it unfold in the exact way you pictured. That is co-creation.

OBSTACLES ARE QUALIFIERS, NOT STOP SIGNS

One of the most important skills you will ever develop is learning how to read obstacles correctly. Most people interpret obstacles as evidence that they are off track.

A door closes, and they think, "This must not be meant for me."

A delay stretches, and they think, "I must have done something wrong."

A challenge arises, and they think, "Maybe I misread everything."

But obstacles are not punishments. They are qualifiers. An obstacle is life asking, *How committed are you really?* A delay is life asking, *Are you anchored, or are you outcome-dependent?* A redirection is life asking, *Can you adapt without collapsing?*

Obstacles refine you. They don't reject you.

They expose where your identity is still fragile.

They reveal where your nervous system still equates uncertainty with danger.

They show you where your attachment is louder than your alignment.

And this matters because when you misread an obstacle as a stop sign, you abandon momentum. But when you read it as a qualifier, you stay in motion. You don't push blindly.

You don't quit dramatically. You adjust. That adjustment is intelligence, not weakness.

You update your strategy without abandoning your vision. You strengthen your identity without shrinking your desire. That is trust in action.

THE WHISPER, THE TAP, AND THE SLAP

Now let's talk about where surrender gets misused most often: when you call it "trust," but your nervous system has actually gone offline. Life is always communicating, but it does so in stages. First comes the whisper. Then the tap. Then the slap.

Some people call it the feather, the brick, and the truck. It's the same idea. At first, life whispers.

A quiet feeling that something is off. A subtle nudge you keep ignoring. A tension in your body when you say yes to something you meant to say no to. An intuitive pull in a direction that doesn't make logical sense. If you don't listen, the whisper becomes a tap.

A repeated pattern.

A small disruption.

A conversation that rattles you.

A door that won't quite open.

An opportunity that feels almost right, but not fully aligned.

If you still don't listen, the tap becomes a slap.

A breakdown.

A loss.

A forced pause.

A situation you cannot ignore.

This is not life punishing you. This is life redirecting you. The goal of surrender is to listen at the whisper stage so that you don't have to learn through the slap. But listening does not mean stopping. It means responding consciously. It means saying, *Something here feels misaligned. Let me adjust.* It means choosing correction instead of collapse.

A CASE STUDY OF MISREAD TRUST

I once worked with a woman who told me, "I'm surrendering." But what she had actually done was disengage.

She stopped taking action.

She stopped following through.

She stopped initiating opportunities.

She stopped reaching out.

She stopped risking.

She said she was trusting. But her nervous system was frozen. When we slowed it down, the truth surfaced. She was not trusting. She was protecting herself from disappointment.

She had been hurt before. She had hoped before. She had taken bold steps before. And when things didn't unfold the way she expected, her system interpreted that as danger.

So, she pulled her energy back. Not in wisdom. In self-protection. That is not surrender. That is bracing. Real trust would have looked like this: Continuing to move while loosening the grip on outcome. Continuing to show up without demanding immediate proof. Continuing to risk without insisting on certainty. When she learned that distinction, everything shifted. She didn't double her effort. She didn't force outcomes. She simply re-engaged.

She took the next aligned step in front of her.

She stopped scanning for confirmation.

She stopped measuring every delay as a verdict.

She began responding to what was real instead of reacting to what she feared. And life met her there. Not instantly. But steadily. When your nervous system is regulated and your energy is open, you can actually recognize opportunity when it appears.

Trust is not waiting for life to prove itself. Trust is remaining in relationship with what is unfolding. It is staying available. It is continuing to participate. It is adjusting without dramatizing. It is believing that a detour does not equal defeat. When surrender becomes stalling, you shrink. When surrender becomes receptivity, you expand. And expansion is what manifestation requires. Not force. Not collapse. Participation. Open hands. Steady feet. And the willingness to move, even when you don't control the map. That is trust without stalling. And that is where manifestation becomes mature.

Trusting the Long Game

One of the reasons surrender feels so threatening is that most people think in short timelines. They think in wins and losses. In proof and no proof. In immediate feedback. But life is not a short game. Life is a long game. And manifestation, when done consciously, is long-term self-leadership. You might lose a battle. You do not lose the war.

Unless you stop.

This is where people get tripped up. They experience disappointment and interpret it as failure. They experience a delay and interpret it as rejection. They experience redirection and interpret it as proof that they were wrong. But disappointment only wins if you stop moving.

Disappointment is not the end. It is a data point. It tells you something didn't align this way. Not that it will never align. The long game requires perspective. And perspective is a nervous system skill. When your system is regulated, you can zoom out. When your system is dysregulated, everything feels final.

Trusting the long game means you don't make permanent decisions from temporary emotions. It means you remember that seasons change. There are seasons of planting and seasons of tending. There are seasons of visible growth and seasons where everything looks still, but roots are strengthening underground. If you judge your life in a planting season as if it should already be ready to harvest, you will convince yourself that something is wrong.

Nothing is wrong. You are mid-cycle.

THE DIFFERENCE BETWEEN A SETBACK AND A DEAD END

A setback asks you to adjust. A dead end asks you to let go. Most people treat setbacks like dead ends.

They hear one "no" and assume it means "never." They encounter one obstacle and assume it means "not meant for me." They feel one wave of doubt and assume it means "I misread everything." But life often says, "not like this," rather than "not at all."

There is a profound difference. A setback refines your approach. A dead end redirects your path. A setback strengthens your identity. A dead end reshapes your vision.

If you collapse at the first "no," you will never reach the "yes" that required the detour. Trusting the long game means you don't catastrophize temporary outcomes. You stay in leadership. You stay curious. You keep showing up. You ask: Is this asking me to quit? Or is this asking me to adjust? That question alone can change your trajectory.

One of the most important distinctions you will learn in this work is the difference between resistance and intuition. Resistance is noisy. It is urgent. It is fear-based. It tries to keep you exactly where you are.

Resistance says: This is uncomfortable. Stop. This might not work. Retreat. This feels scary. Abort.

Intuition is different. It is calm. It is spacious. It does not argue. It nudges rather than pushes.

Intuition feels like clarity without panic. Resistance feels like panic disguised as wisdom.

When people say, "I followed my intuition and stopped," what they often mean is, "I felt uncomfortable and interpreted that as a sign to retreat."

The 24/7 Manifestation Method trains you to regulate before you decide. Because if you confuse resistance for intuition, you will keep abandoning yourself at the exact moment growth begins. Alignment does not always feel easy at first. But it does feel true. It feels steady, not frantic. It feels expansive, not constricted. When your nervous system is regulated, you can hear intuition clearly. When it is dysregulated, fear gets the microphone. Trusting the long game requires that you pause long enough to tell the difference.

THE DANGER OF WAITING FOR CERTAINTY

Certainty does not precede change. Change creates certainty. If you wait to feel fully confident before acting, you will wait forever. Confidence is not a prerequisite. It is a byproduct.

Many people say they are "waiting for clarity." What they are often waiting for is the absence of fear. But fear does not disappear before growth.

It quiets after evidence. And evidence comes from movement.

The 24/7 Manifestation Method does not ask you to leap blindly. It asks you to move gently and consistently.

One aligned action.

One regulated response.

One boundary.

One brave step.

Trust is not built in dramatic leaps but in steady follow-through.

INNER AUTHORITY AND THE SOVEREIGN SELF

There comes a point in this work where external validation begins to lose its grip. It's not because you no longer care about other people, but because you have developed inner authority. Your sovereign self. This is the part of you that can make decisions without waiting for permission. This part of you can stay anchored even when opinions vary, the part that trusts its own discernment. This is what surrender matures into.

Not obedience. Sovereignty.

You are no longer asking life to tell you who you are. You are moving from self-trust and letting life collaborate. That is the difference between childish faith and adult trust. Childish faith says, "If it works, I'll believe." Adult trust says, "I will show up consistently, and I trust myself to respond to what unfolds." That level of inner authority stabilizes your nervous system. It removes the frantic need for constant confirmation. It allows you to walk forward without scanning for approval at every step.

Trust is not tested when things are going well. Trust is tested when the timeline stretches.

The outcome changes. The feedback is unclear. The excitement fades. The work continues quietly without applause.

This is where trust becomes embodied, not performative.

Embodied trust sounds like:

"I don't know how this will unfold, but I know how I will show up."

"I can stay present without certainty."

"I can adapt without abandoning myself."

"I can want this without collapsing if it shifts."

That level of trust stabilizes your nervous system. And a regulated nervous system receives more clearly. You recognize opportunity instead of missing it. You interpret obstacles accurately instead of catastrophizing. You adjust without spiraling. You remain available.

The long game is not about blind optimism. It is about sustained leadership. It is about refusing to let temporary discomfort rewrite your identity. It is about understanding that growth is cyclical. It is about remembering that alignment is not measured in days. It is measured in seasons. When you trust the long game, you stop reacting to every fluctuation. You stop turning pauses into verdicts. You stop letting one disappointment define your future. You remain steady. And steadiness is magnetic because life responds to coherence. And coherence over time creates inevitability. Trusting the long game means you do not rush your becoming. You participate in it. You regulate through it. You lead yourself through it. And in doing so, you build a life that is not just reactive to circumstances but resilient within them. That is not naïve hope. That is embodied power. And that is what makes manifestation sustainable.

Let's normalize disappointment. Disappointment does not mean you were foolish to hope. It means you cared. It means you showed up with an open heart. It means you were willing to want something. And caring is not a liability. It is a strength.

The problem is not disappointment.

The problem is when disappointment becomes identity.

When one outcome turns into a story: "I'm always let down." "This never works." "Maybe I just shouldn't want things." That is the moment momentum collapses. Not because the desire was wrong, but because the narrative hardened.

Disappointment is an emotional wave. Identity is a decision. You are allowed to feel the wave. You are not required to become it. Instead of numbing disappointment or shaming yourself for feeling it, process it. Name it. Breathe through it. Ask what it revealed.

Did it expose an attachment?

A timeline you were gripping?

An expectation that needed loosening?

Then keep going. Because the only way disappointment wins is if it convinces you to withdraw your participation. And participation is your power. You are not weak for wanting. You are brave. And brave people feel deeply and continue anyway.

The Surrender Sweet Spot

There is a place in this work where effort softens, but momentum does not disappear. It is not the frantic energy of proving. It is not the collapsed energy of "whatever." It is the steady, grounded rhythm of co-creation. The surrender sweet spot is where action and trust meet.

It feels like this:

You take the aligned step.

You send the email.

You have the conversation.

You apply.

You publish.

You show up.

And then you unclench. You release the demand that it must unfold in a specific way, on a specific timeline, through a specific person. You stay open to feedback instead of interpreting every response as a verdict on your worth. You adjust without dramatizing. You respond without spiraling.

You trust yourself to handle what comes next. This is not passive. It is responsive.

In the beginning of a manifestation journey, most people swing between extremes. They either grip so tightly that they suffocate the process, or they detach so quickly that they abandon it. They mistake intensity for commitment and indifference for surrender. But the sweet spot lives in the middle.

It is powerful without being forceful. It is hopeful without being desperate. It is committed without being rigid. And this is where manifestation becomes fluid because you are no longer trying to control life. You are dancing with it. When you are in this sweet spot, your nervous system is regulated enough to receive. You are not bracing against disappointment. You are not micromanaging outcomes. You are not interpreting silence as rejection. You are participating fully and releasing cleanly. This is coherence in motion. And coherence accelerates everything.

The Sign Practice: Your Personal Yes

One of the simplest ways to strengthen surrender without slipping into passivity is to give your nervous system a gentle way to register, *I'm supported.* Not because you need proof in order to keep going, but because the human mind loves feedback. When you are learning to trust, small moments of reassurance help your body relax. And when your body relaxes, you stop gripping. And when you stop gripping, you can actually receive.

So here is your practice for the next seven days.

Choose one sign.

It can be a number, a symbol, or a pattern that feels neutral and easy to notice. 111. A butterfly. A white feather. A specific word. A song title. A color that keeps appearing. Keep it simple. Choose something that does not require you to hunt or overthink. Then, for the next week, write it in your journal twice a day.

Morning:

> "Today, I am open to being guided. Show me my sign if I am on the right path."

Night:

> "Where did I see support today? Where did I feel led, protected, or redirected?"

This is the part that matters. You are not asking for the sign as a demand.

Not:

> "If I don't see it, I should panic."
>
> "If it doesn't show up by Tuesday, this isn't meant for me."
>
> "If I see it three times, I must make a huge decision."

That is control disguised as spirituality. You are asking for reassurance, not negotiation. You are practicing relationship. And here is the rule that keeps this clean: I don't chase the sign. I receive it.

If you notice yourself scanning obsessively, refreshing your phone, reading into everything, pause. Take a breath. Come back to the surrender sweet spot. Aligned action plus open hands. Signs are not meant to replace your inner authority. They are not meant to make decisions for you. They are not shortcuts around discernment. They are gentle nudges.

They soften your grip. They remind you that life is interactive. They train your nervous system to notice support instead of scanning for threat. And over time, something subtle shifts. You stop looking for proof that it won't work. You start noticing evidence that you are held. That shift alone changes how you move.

The Fastest Way to Speed This Up

Manifestations do not slow down because the universe is confused. They slow down where you are internally divided. Every desire carries a frequency. And every contradiction creates drag.

You say you want love. But you rehearse unworthiness.

You overanalyze texts. You brace for abandonment.

You keep one foot emotionally out the door.

You say you want money. But you fear responsibility.

You fear being seen. You fear judgment.

You associate wealth with pressure, isolation, or loss of freedom.

You say you want expansion. But you protect the identity that kept you small.

You cling to the story of being overlooked.

You stay loyal to the version of you who survived by shrinking.

You say you want visibility. But you are still emotionally invested in anonymity.

You want to be seen but not criticized. Heard, but not challenged.

Celebrated, but not misunderstood.

This is not hypocrisy. It is conditioning.

And manifestation slows down anywhere there is an internal "no" running beneath your conscious "yes." This is why surrender is not just external.

It is not just:

"I release the timeline."

"I let go of control."

"I trust divine timing."

It is also:

"I release the belief that I cannot safely hold what I am asking for."

Surrender removes the chokehold. But it also removes the internal contradiction.

This is where the Four Pillars return.

Mindset clears the belief.

Emotion regulates the fear.

Identity upgrades the self-concept.

Aligned action creates new evidence.

When those four are coherent, acceleration happens naturally.

You do not speed things up by pushing harder. You speed things up by removing resistance inside yourself. You do not force expansion. You become safe for expansion.

You do not chase love. You become available for love.

You do not grip money. You become congruent with receiving it.

This is the turbo boost. Not force. Coherence. When nothing inside you is arguing with the desire, the delay dissolves. And suddenly, what felt stuck begins to move. Not because you wrestled it into place.

But because you stopped resisting it from within. That is the surrender sweet spot. Aligned action. Open hands. Internal agreement. And when you live there, manifestation stops feeling like effort. It feels like flow.

A Practice for Trust Without Stalling

There will be moments when surrender feels suspiciously similar to quitting. Moments when you are tired. Moments when progress feels slow. Moments when your ego whispers, "Maybe I should just let this go." And sometimes that voice is wisdom.

But sometimes it is self-protection. This is why discernment matters.

When you feel tempted to "surrender" by pulling back completely, pause before you withdraw your energy. Ask yourself, slowly and honestly: Am I releasing control, or am I avoiding disappointment? Am I staying open, or am I shutting down? What is one aligned action I can still take without forcing an outcome?

These questions interrupt autopilot.

Avoidance wants relief. Trust wants clarity. Avoidance says, "If I stop caring, it won't hurt."

Trust says, "I can care without gripping." Avoidance collapses your energy.

Trust keeps it circulating. So instead of making a dramatic decision, choose one small action that keeps you in relationship with your desire.

Send the follow-up email.

Update the portfolio.

Have the honest conversation.

Revisit the application.

Show up for the call.

Write the post.

Small. Clean. Intentional.

No performance. No pressure. No demand that it must work immediately. Just movement.

That is trust in motion. The key is this: you are not acting to control the outcome. You are acting to stay congruent with who you are becoming. This keeps your nervous system engaged instead of frozen. It prevents surrender from turning into stalling. It reminds your subconscious that you are still participating, even while you are releasing attachment.

Trust does not require grand gestures. It requires consistency. One aligned action keeps the channel open. And open channels receive.

Trust is not silence. It is conversation.

You speak through your actions.

Life responds through experience.

You listen.

You adjust.

You respond again.

That exchange is ongoing. When you disengage, the conversation stops. When you harden, the channel narrows. When you grip, the signal distorts. But when you stay present, even without answers, the dialogue continues. Trust is not a mood. It is not something you feel once and then possess forever. It is a way of moving through uncertainty, a posture, a rhythm.

You move.

You release.

You observe.

You refine.

That is surrender. Not stepping back from your desire, but stepping out of the chokehold. You are no longer demanding proof before you proceed. You are no longer withholding participation until certainty arrives. You are walking forward and allowing reality to meet you there. This is mature manifestation.

Not frantic.

Not passive.

Responsive.

And responsive people evolve quickly. They are not arguing with feedback; they are integrating it. In the next chapter, we will take this embodied trust and apply it to something very specific: how to manifest what you want without gripping it so tightly that you block its arrival.

We will talk about what it looks like to live from trust long term, how surrender stabilizes your identity instead of destabilizing it, and how to know when it is time to rest and when it is time to move.

It's not through guesswork but through discernment. Trust is not blind. It is intelligent. And once you learn to live from it, your entire relationship with manifestation changes.

Closing: Making the Shift

You have now moved through something that most people never fully commit to. Not just learning or thinking differently, but practicing, noticing, interrupting, and choosing, again and again.

And whether it felt smooth or messy, clear or confronting, powerful or subtle, something has shifted. Maybe it's the way you catch your thoughts more quickly. Maybe it's how you respond instead of react. Maybe it's the quiet awareness that you are no longer moving through your day unconsciously.

Manifestation is not built in the big, dramatic moments. It is built in these small, repeated decisions, the ones no one else sees, the ones that slowly become who you are. Over these past days, you have begun creating a new internal rhythm. And once that rhythm begins, your system starts to recognize it as familiar. Safe. Available.

This is how change lasts. Not because you forced it. But because you practiced it enough that it started to feel like you. And that is the shift from doing to becoming.

But this is not the end of the work. It is the beginning of living it. The goal was never to complete a seven-day process and go back to how things were. The goal was to create a new way of relating to yourself … that continues.

In the next chapter, we'll move beyond the structure of the method and into what it means to sustain this in your real life. How to carry this awareness forward. How to continue choosing alignment without needing perfect conditions. And how to allow this way of being to evolve with you, instead of feeling like something you have to maintain, because this doesn't end here. This is where it becomes yours.

Reflection Questions

Take a few moments to reflect, either in your mind or by writing your responses down. There is no right answer here, only awareness.

1. What has shifted in me over the past seven days, even in small ways?
2. When did I notice myself choosing differently than I normally would?
3. What patterns or reactions became more visible to me?
4. Where did I feel the most aligned with my future self?
5. Where did I feel resistance, and what might that be showing me?
6. What felt natural during this process, and what felt unfamiliar?
7. How has my relationship with my thoughts, emotions, or actions changed?

CHAPTER 8

Manifesting Money, Love, and Success

For a long time, I believed manifestation worked best when I didn't want too much. I would soften my desires. Downplay them. Keep them abstract enough that I could never be fully disappointed. I told myself I was being spiritual. Detached. Evolved.

What I was actually doing was protecting myself from clarity.

Clarity makes things real. And when something is real, it can be lost. It can fail. It can expose you. So, I hid behind vague language. "I just want to be happy." "I'm open to whatever." "I don't want to be too attached." But underneath those words was a quieter truth:

I was afraid to hope boldly and not receive.

If you've ever diluted your desire to make it safer, you are not weak. You are human. Your nervous system was trying to protect you from disappointment. But protection is not the same as alignment.

This chapter is about reclaiming your right to want clearly. To name the number. To define the relationship. To articulate the impact. Not so you can control the outcome, but so you can orient your identity. Clarity is not the opposite of surrender. Clarity is what makes surrender intelligent.

Why Clarity Comes Before Results

There is a truth that sounds almost too simple, yet it changes everything: the first step to being on the path is knowing what you want. Not what you *should* want. Not what sounds reasonable. Not what feels safe enough to admit.

What you want.

Many people think they're manifesting when they're actually circling ambiguity. They say: "I just want to be happy." "I just want abundance." "I just want love." "I just want success."

But the subconscious mind doesn't work with abstractions. It works with direction. And direction requires clarity. Clarity is not pressure. Clarity is orientation. It tells your nervous system where you're going so it can stop bracing in every direction at once.

Here's what's also true: the moment you get clear, your mind will want to jump straight to the logistics. How will it happen? When will it happen? Who will help? What if it doesn't work? That's normal. The brain looks for certainty before it looks for possibility.

But the "how" doesn't unlock until the desire is honest enough to create momentum. Your job is not to force the answer. Your job is to tell the truth about the direction. The rest reveals itself in motion.

The Law of Specificity (Without Rigidity)

There is a quiet law that governs manifestation, whether you acknowledge it or not:

> …the more specific your desire, the cleaner the signal. This does not mean obsessing over details. It means giving your subconscious something to orient toward. Vague desires create scattered energy. Specific desires create coherence.

Specific does not mean controlling. It means clear.

Instead of saying: "I want more money."

Clarity sounds like: "I want to earn $10,000 a month doing work that feels meaningful and spacious."

Instead of saying: "I want love."

Clarity sounds like: "I want a relationship where I feel emotionally safe, chosen, and able to be fully myself."

Instead of saying: "I want success."

Clarity sounds like: "I want to lead work that impacts people and supports my family without burning me out."

This is not about being demanding. It's about being honest. And honesty is magnetic. When you can name what you want without apologizing for it, you stop leaking energy through indecision. You stop negotiating with your own desire. You stop performing vagueness to avoid disappointment.

You become available.

Clarity sets the destination. Surrender releases the grip. And the method you've built in the previous chapters is what keeps you regulated enough to walk toward what you chose. Now we're going to take that clarity and bring it into the three areas that tend to trigger the most charge in people's nervous systems: money, love, and success. Not as abstract ideas, but as lived realities.

It's one thing to want clearly. It's another to regulate your way into receiving it. Let's apply the method.

Before we go any further, here's the point of this chapter: you are not going to "think" your way into money, love, or success. You are going to *practice* your way into them.

So, each section below will give you three things:

1. A nervous-system reframe
2. A set of 24/7 tools tailored to that area
3. Real scripts, affirmations, and simple rituals you can actually use

Your nervous system needs a *felt* destination, not just a logical one.

Clarity becomes powerful when you can recognize it in your body and your life. Not as perfection, but as signals: steadier breath, cleaner decisions, less urgency, more self-trust. Measurable does not mean shallow; it means recognizable. If you cannot recognize what you asked for when it arrives, you cannot stabilize it.

Your job is to define the "what" with honesty. Life's job is to reveal the "how" through timing, people, and unexpected routes.

That combination is not passive. It is mature. Now let's bring that clarity into the three areas that tend to activate the most charge: money, love, and success.

It makes you aware. And awareness, when grounded in self-trust, is one of the most powerful forces in manifestation.

MONEY (CAREFULLY FRAMED): A NEUTRAL CONVERSATION

Let's talk about money in a way that is clean, grounded, and empowering. Money is not moral.

Money is not spiritual or unspiritual. Money is not proof that you are good, bad, worthy, unworthy, evolved, or behind.

Money Is a Tool, a Symbol, a Translator of Choice

And for most of us, money represents freedom.

Freedom to choose.

Freedom to rest.

Freedom to support others without depletion.

Freedom to leave what no longer fits.

Freedom to invest in what makes you feel alive.

That's why money brings up so much. Not because money is heavy, but because freedom is charged. Freedom asks your nervous system questions. Freedom asks your identity questions. Freedom asks your history questions. The problems that arise around money rarely come from money itself. They come from the conditioning around it.

Money responds to the story your body believes, not the story your mouth repeats. So, we start by cleaning up the signal.

1. **Scarcity-to-abundance language (script you will actually use)**

   Replace phrases that train your nervous system to brace.
   - "I can't afford that" becomes "That's not aligned right now, and I'm expanding my capacity to receive."
   - "Money is tight" becomes "Money is circulating, and I'm strengthening my relationship with support."
   - "I'm broke" becomes "I'm in the process of building wealth."
   - "This bill stresses me out" becomes "This is information. I can respond with clarity."

2. **Daily money gratitude (two minutes, no performance)**
   Each day, write the following:
   - Three things you paid for that supported you.
   - Three experiences money made possible.
   - One line of appreciation, such as: "Money supports me in visible and invisible ways."

   This trains your system to associate money with support instead of threat.
3. **Identify and reframe the belief (mindset tool)**
   Finish this sentence: "If I had more money, then ...."

   Whatever you write next is usually the fear. Reframe it with a sentence your body can grow into:
   - "I don't have to choose between wealth and peace. I get both."
   - "I am safe with more."
   - "Ease is allowed in my life."
4. **Treat money with respect (Aligned Action ritual)**
   Pick one small ritual that signals safety to your subconscious:
   - Organize your wallet, remove receipts, make space.
   - Open your bank account once a day with curiosity, not panic.
   - Unsubscribe from financial clutter you do not need.
   - Choose one money action you avoid (invoice, budget, follow-up) and do it calmly.

   Money does not need you to worship it. It needs you to stop treating it like an emergency.
5. **Embody the financially free version of you (identity tool)**
   Ask: "What would the resourced version of me do today?"

   Then choose one action from that identity: a cleaner boundary, a better decision, a braver ask, a more honest conversation.

Money Affirmations (Say One Daily, Not All Twelve)

- "I am open to receiving money from expected and unexpected sources."
- "Wealth flows to me because I am aligned."
- "I honor and attract money with ease and joy."
- "I am safe holding more."

This is not about forcing money to arrive. It's about becoming coherent with the life that can hold it.

Many people carry subconscious beliefs:

"Money creates stress."

"Money disappears."

"More money means more responsibility."

"I can't relax if I have more."

"Money changes people."

"If I have more, someone will want something from me."

"If I have more, I might lose it."

"If I have more, I'll have to become someone I don't like."

These beliefs do not make you bad. They make you conditioned. And conditioning can be updated. Here is the truth: money does not block expansion. Beliefs about money do. If your system learned that money equals pressure, your body will resist it, even if your mind says you want abundance. If your system learned that money equals conflict, your body will brace the moment you check your account. If your system learned that money equals instability, you will unconsciously recreate instability because it feels familiar.

So manifesting money is not about becoming someone else. It's about becoming safe for money.

Safe to receive it.

Safe to hold it.

Safe to manage it.

Safe to enjoy it.

Safe to let it support you without guilt.

This is where the Four Pillars show up again, quietly and powerfully.

Mindset: you identify and reframe the belief.

Emotion: you regulate the fear that belief is protecting.

Identity: you become the version of you who expects support, not struggle.

Aligned action: you treat money with respect in real time, even before you have more of it.

When money feels safer, it flows more easily. Not because the universe rewards you for "being good," but because you stop resisting it. You stop sending mixed signals. You stop tightening around the very thing you are asking to enter. And you can start with tiny, neutral actions that retrain your system: checking your bank account with curiosity instead of panic, organizing your wallet like you're making space for support, speaking about money in a way that doesn't reinforce scarcity. These actions are not magical; they are signals. And your subconscious listens to signals more than it listens to speeches.

SUCCESS WITHOUT SELF-BETRAYAL

Success is another loaded word. For many people, success is subconsciously linked to burnout, pressure, visibility without protection, responsibility without support, and being needed more than being nourished.

They want success, and fear it at the same time. That creates mixed signals. Clarity here is essential. What kind of success do you want?

Not culturally impressive success.

Not performative success.

Aligned success.

Success that supports your nervous system.

Success that allows rest.

Success that feels sustainable.

Success that aligns with your values.

Success that doesn't cost your peace.

You are allowed to define success on your terms. In fact, you must. Otherwise, your subconscious will sabotage what it associates with danger.

LOVE BEGINS WITH EMOTIONAL CLARITY

Love responds to clarity too. Not a checklist. Clarity.

Clarity about how you want to feel.

Clarity about how you want to be treated.

Clarity about what safety looks like for you.

Clarity about what you're no longer willing to tolerate.

This is not about controlling another person. It's about knowing yourself well enough to recognize alignment. Vague longing attracts vague experiences. Clear emotional standards attract resonance.

INTEGRATION PRACTICE: CLARITY WITHOUT FORCE

Take your journal. Write three headings:

Money

Love

Success

Under each, answer these questions honestly:

- What do I want to experience here?
- How do I want to feel in my body when this is present?
- What outdated belief might make this feel unsafe?
- What am I responsible for clarifying?
- What am I willing to release control over?

Do not rush this. This is not about perfection. This is about precision.

Permission to Want

You do not need to earn the right to want more. You do not need to prove you are grateful before you ask for expansion. You do not need to minimize your desires to be spiritual.

You do not need to pretend you are "above" money, love, or success in order to be evolved.

For many of us, wanting was complicated early. We were taught to be content. To not ask for too much. To not be "greedy." To not be dramatic. To not be unrealistic. So, we learned to edit ourselves. We softened our dreams. We made them smaller, safer, and more socially acceptable.

Desire is not ego. Desire is direction.

Desire is the language of expansion. It is how your future self communicates with your present self. It is how life nudges you forward. When you feel the pull toward more love, more ease, more impact, that is not selfish. It is growth. You are allowed to want clearly and trust deeply at the same time.

That combination is powerful.

Clarity without surrender becomes control.

Surrender without clarity becomes passivity.

But clarity with trust becomes alignment.

And alignment changes everything.

The moment you get honest about what you want, everything inside you that believes you cannot have it starts to speak up. Not to sabotage you. To protect you. This is where money, love, and success stop being abstract ideas and start touching your nervous system, your history, and your identity. This is where manifestation becomes embodied.

The moment you define your desire clearly, one of two things usually happens. Either you feel relief, or you feel fear. Sometimes you feel both at the same time. Relief because something inside you finally feels seen. Fear because clarity removes the illusion of distance. Vague dreams are safe. Specific desires are confrontational.

When you say, "I want abundance," your system nods politely.

When you say, "I want to earn $20,000 a month doing work I love," your system leans forward and asks questions.

When you say, "I want love," nothing trembles.

When you say, "I want a relationship where I am fully seen and emotionally safe," your nervous system checks the archives.

Specificity activates memory. It asks:

What if this actually happens?

Who would I need to become to hold this?

What would I lose if I succeeded?

What would change if I stopped struggling?

Resistance is not a sign that you chose the wrong desire. It is a sign you chose a real one.

The Nervous System's Relationship with Expansion

Here is something that will save you years of self-judgment: Your nervous system does not evaluate desires based on logic. It evaluates them based on safety.

If your system associates money with stress, more money feels unsafe. If it associates love with abandonment, deeper intimacy feels unsafe. If it associates success with pressure, visibility feels unsafe.

So, when clarity arrives, the nervous system checks the archives.

Have we survived this before?

Did this hurt last time?

Did this overwhelm us?

Did this cost us love, rest, or belonging?

If the answer is yes, resistance appears. Not to stop you. To slow you down enough to renegotiate safety. That renegotiation is where manifestation becomes embodied instead of imagined. Without it, you might attract something briefly but lose it because your system cannot stabilize it. With it, you expand at a pace your body can sustain.

Money will always press on your relationship with freedom. That does not mean you are doing it wrong. It means money touches history, identity, and safety.

So, when resistance shows up here, do not shame it. Translate it. Ask, "What consequence is my body afraid of?" Then use the practices above to teach your system: "More can be safe."

It starts feeling supportive.

This is permission to want more without shame. Permission to expand without apology. Permission to build a life that feels resourced instead of restricted.

Desire is not your enemy. Unexamined fear is. And when you meet that fear with regulation, clarity, and compassion, you do not have to shrink your dreams. You simply become safe enough to hold them.

Love: When Desire Meets Vulnerability

Love is often the desire people are most vague about, not because they don't want it, but because they've been hurt. So, they soften the ask.

They say,

"I just want someone nice."

"I just want peace."

"I just don't want drama."

But that isn't clarity. That's damage control. Clarity in love is not about avoiding pain. It's about defining safety. It asks questions like:

How do I want to feel emotionally in this relationship?

What kind of communication allows my body to relax?

What does consistency look like for me?

What behaviors make my nervous system feel secure instead of hypervigilant?

This kind of clarity can feel terrifying because it removes your ability to settle unconsciously. And settling often feels safer than risking disappointment. When you are vague, you can tolerate almost anything. When you are clear, you must walk away from what does not align.

So, when you get honest about love, resistance often surfaces in subtle ways: Attraction to unavailable people. Boredom with healthy options. Fear of being fully seen. Over-independence disguised as strength. Self-sufficiency as armor.

These are not character flaws. They are adaptations. Your nervous system learned them to protect you. But protection is not the same as intimacy. Love requires internal permission. Many people believe love will heal their wounds. But love first asks you to look at them.

It asks:

Are you willing to be seen without hiding?

Are you willing to receive without earning?

Are you willing to trust without controlling?

That is vulnerable work. Because if you have equated love with abandonment, betrayal, or instability, your system may brace the moment something feels steady. Stability can feel foreign. Calm can feel suspicious.

Clarity forces the identity shift.

Who are you without the armor?

Who are you when you do not have to brace?

Who are you when love does not require struggle to feel meaningful?

These questions are not meant to destabilize you. They are meant to prepare you to hold what you are asking for. Love does not respond to perfection. It responds to coherence. When your desire for love is clear and your nervous system feels safe enough to receive it, you stop chasing chemistry that mirrors chaos. You start choosing resonance that mirrors regulation.

LOVE PRACTICES: CLARITY THAT CREATES SAFETY

1. **The "felt standards" script (not a checklist)**
   Write this and read it daily for seven days:
   "In love, I am available for consistency, emotional safety, honesty, and repair. I am no longer available for confusion, hiding, hot and cold, or potential without follow-through."
2. **Your nervous system yes (standards you can recognize)**
   Answer in your journal:
   - "My body feels safe in love when …."
   - "My body braces in love when …."
   - "The version of me who receives secure love does not …."
3. **The communication ritual (two minutes before you text)**
   Before you send an anxious message, pause and do this:
   - One hand on your chest.
   - One slow inhale, longer exhale.

   Ask: "Am I reaching for connection or reaching for certainty?"
   - Then respond from connection.
4. **Love affirmations (one at a time, let them land)**
   - "Love can be calm and still be real."
   - "I am safe being seen."
   - "I receive love without earning it."
   - "I choose partners who choose me back."
5. **The identity shift (the real manifestation work)**

Each day, choose one action that proves you are no longer negotiating your worth: a boundary, a truth spoken kindly, a pattern you refuse to repeat.

From Guarded to Open

Then there was Penelope. After a painful divorce in her twenties, her nervous system learned:

"Love is dangerous."

"Trust leads to humiliation."

"Guard yourself."

She believed, deeply, that everyone cheats and that she wasn't lovable. During the 24/7 Manifestation Method, she wasn't trying to manifest a partner. She was building safety around love. She shifted from "everyone cheats" to "I choose integrity." From "I'm not lovable" to "I am love."

She didn't shift through forced positivity but through repetition, regulation, and embodiment. Her body softened around intimacy. Her identity expanded. Her standards became clear. Not long after, she reconnected with someone from her past. But this time, she saw him without armor. Without fear. Without bracing. They fell in love. She invited me to her wedding. Her relationship didn't change because she found the "right" person. It changed because she became the version of herself who could receive secure love.

Money, love, and success are not external trophies. They are reflections of internal coherence. And you are already building it, one aligned decision at a time.

Success: Visibility, Responsibility, and Identity

Success can feel just as vulnerable as love. Not because you do not want it, but because success changes how you are perceived. It increases visibility. It raises expectations. It brings responsibility.

So, when you define success clearly, your system may quietly ask:

Will I still be allowed to rest?

Will I still be loved?

Will people resent me?

Will I have to perform forever?

This is why people unconsciously cap their success. Not because they lack ambition, but because they fear the cost. Clarity gives you the opportunity to redefine success before it arrives, to separate aligned success from inherited definitions. Aligned success feels different from performative success.

Aligned success

allows space,

includes rest,

feels sustainable,

honors boundaries, and

does not require constant proving.

When you define success this way, your system relaxes. And relaxed systems expand more easily. Success does not have to mean burnout. Visibility does not have to mean exposure without safety. Responsibility does not have to mean self-betrayal. You are allowed to design success that supports your nervous system instead of destabilizing it.

Case Study: The Career Shift That Came Through Persistence

A client of mine, Miriam, knew she wanted a new career but couldn't see the path forward. She felt stuck in her role and doubted her qualifications for anything else.

Her beliefs were loud:

"I'm not qualified."

"It's too competitive."

"I should just be grateful."

During the 24/7 Manifestation Method, she didn't magically discover a flawless plan. She uncovered the identity that kept her small. We worked on mindset. We regulated fear. We updated her self-concept. She continued applying. She continued showing up. She did not wait for certainty.

She stayed engaged without gripping. And eventually, she landed the role she had quietly hoped for. Not because the universe dropped it into her lap, but because her internal resistance stopped blocking her movement. Manifestation met her halfway.

SUCCESS PRACTICES: VISIBILITY WITHOUT SELF-BETRAYAL

1. **Redefine success in one sentence (so your body stops resisting it)**
   "Success, for me, is __________, and it includes rest, boundaries, and sustainability."
2. **Visibility regulation script (use before you post, pitch, or lead)**
   "It is safe to be seen. I do not have to perform to be loved. I can lead from steadiness. I can expand without abandoning myself."
3. **The "clean action" ritual (aligned action)**

Choose one success move per day that you do calmly, without urgency:

Send the email

Submit the proposal

Publish the post

Raise the rate

Practice the talk

The nervous system learns success is safe through repetition, not hype.

Use these success affirmations:

"I am safe with greater responsibility."

"My work is impactful and sustainable."

"I can be visible and protected."

"I expand at the pace I can hold."

Resistance Is Information, Not Opposition

When resistance shows up after clarity, do not treat it as an enemy. Resistance is rarely sabotage. It is communication.

Often it is saying:

"I don't feel safe yet."

"I need reassurance."

"I need a slower pace."

"I need proof that I won't be abandoned."

If you try to bulldoze resistance, you create internal conflict. But if you meet it with curiosity, you create integration.

Ask gently:

What is this part protecting?

What memory is being activated?

What would help this feel safer?

What is one small step that keeps me open without overwhelming me?

This is how clarity becomes embodied instead of aspirational. You are not here to override your nervous system. You are here to collaborate with it. When love and success feel safe in your body, not just inspiring in your mind, you stop chasing them from anxiety. You begin receiving them from coherence. And that shift changes everything.

A Story of Money, Love, and Timing

There was a period in my life when I wanted three things at once: More financial ease. Deeper intimacy. Greater impact.

I didn't want them eventually. I wanted them **now**. I had done the mindset work. I had regulated my emotions. I had shifted my identity. I had taken aligned action. So, I assumed they would arrive in a synchronized wave of reward. They didn't.

Life brought them in waves. Not to frustrate me. To prepare me.

Money came first. Not extreme wealth. But noticeable ease: Opportunities that paid well. Clients who felt aligned. Revenue that felt supportive instead of stressful. And what I realized was this: money was teaching me trust.

It was asking, "Can you receive without gripping?"

"Can you see increase without assuming it will disappear?"

"Can you relax when things are working?"

Money wasn't testing my worth. It was upgrading my nervous system's relationship with safety. Then love deepened. Not through drama. Through vulnerability. Through conversations that required honesty instead of performance. Through choosing openness instead of control. And love asked different questions.

"Can you be seen without hiding?"

"Can you receive care without earning it?"

"Can you stay when it's calm instead of manufacturing chaos?"

Love wasn't about finding someone new. It was about becoming someone available. Success arrived last.

And by then, I understood something I hadn't before. Success wasn't about applause. It was about responsibility without self-betrayal. It was about leading without abandoning my nervous system. It was about expansion without burnout. Each desire required a different internal stabilization.

Looking back, I see the wisdom in the sequencing. If success had come before money felt safe, I would have overworked. If love had deepened before I trusted myself financially, I might have attached from scarcity. If impact had expanded before I learned boundaries, I would have drained myself trying to hold it. Clarity didn't speed the process. It made it accurate. It allowed life to bring things in the order my system could sustain.

When Your Why Gets Tested

When clarity is real, your why will be tested. Not because life is cruel, but because growth is precise.

You will be asked:

Do you want this enough to stay present when it's inconvenient?

Do you want this enough to grow beyond your old identity?

Do you want this enough to release the habits that kept you safe but small?

This is not punishment. It is preparation. If your why is surface-level, discomfort will stop you.

If your why is deep, discomfort becomes instruction. That is why reasons come first, and answers come second.

Your why stabilizes you when the how is unclear.

Your why keeps you regulated when timelines stretch.

Your why reminds you who you are becoming when doubt gets loud.

When your reason is shallow, resistance feels like proof to quit. When your reason is grounded, resistance feels like refinement.

The Difference Between Wanting and Chasing

There is a subtle but powerful difference between wanting something and chasing it. Wanting is grounded. Chasing is anxious.

Wanting says: "I know what I desire. I am open to receiving it."

Chasing says: "If this doesn't happen soon, something is wrong with me."

Wanting allows space. Chasing creates pressure.

When clarity is paired with surrender, you remain in wanting. When clarity is paired with control, you slip into chasing. So, when urgency rises, pause.

Ask yourself: What am I afraid will happen if this doesn't arrive yet?

Often the answer is not about the desire itself. It's about a belief underneath.

"If I don't get this soon, I'll fall behind."

"If this doesn't happen, I'll never feel secure."

"If this doesn't work, it means I'm not enough."

Those beliefs can be softened. But only if you see them.

Integrating Clarity into Daily Life

Clarity is not a one-time declaration. It is a lived posture. It shows up in small ways: You say no to what drains you. You stop negotiating your standards. You make financial decisions aligned with your future, not your fear. You speak honestly instead of performing stability. You rest without apologizing. This is how money, love, and success materialize.

Not through dramatic leaps.

Through consistent congruence.

Your subconscious is watching your daily behavior more than your declarations. When your actions reflect your clarity, your system begins to believe you.

A Practice for Working with Resistance

When resistance appears, don't override it. Work with it.

Try this:

Name the desire clearly.

Name the fear without judgment.

Place your hand on your body.

Breathe slowly until the sensation shifts.

Then ask: What would feel like a safe next step?

Not the entire journey.

Just the next step.

Send the message.

Research the option.

Set the boundary.

Apply for the opportunity.

This keeps momentum alive without force. Force overwhelms the nervous system.

Small, aligned steps build capacity.

The Quiet Shift That Signals Alignment

You will know alignment is forming long before dramatic results arrive.

You will notice:

Urgency decreases.

Self-trust increases.

Comparison fades.

Patience feels possible.

Curiosity replaces panic.

These are not small shifts. They are evidence that your internal architecture is changing. When your nervous system stabilizes, your outer world begins to reorganize around that stability.

Letting Clarity Do Its Work

Clarity is not a demand. It is an invitation: An invitation to see where you are ready. An invitation to notice what needs reassurance. An invitation to release outdated protection. Money, love, and success do not arrive because you force them. They arrive when your internal conditions can hold them. Clarity reveals those conditions. And over time, something subtle but profound happens.

Manifestation stops feeling like something you are trying to do. It becomes something you notice. You notice how your body responds to opportunity. You notice how quickly you recover from disappointment. You notice the tone of your inner dialogue when things shift. You notice that you are no longer chasing. You are participating.

Money, love, and success stop living in separate compartments. They begin informing each other. They reflect the same core state: safety, coherence, and self-trust. Because they were never meant to be pursued in isolation. They were always meant to grow from the same foundation. And that foundation is you.

When Money, Love, and Success Start Talking to Each Other

One of the most surprising shifts people experience when they live the 24/7 Manifestation Method consistently is this: progress in one area begins to unlock movement in another.

Money improves, and suddenly, boundaries in relationships feel easier. Love stabilizes, and creative work flows with less resistance. Success expands, and money feels less charged.

At first, it looks like coincidence. It's not.

It's coherence.

Money, love, and success are not separate manifestations. They are expressions of the same internal state. When your nervous system feels safer, your standards rise naturally. When your identity expands, your capacity across domains expands with it. When self-trust deepens, it affects everything.

Nothing is siloed. Your inner world is always communicating across domains.

If you distrust yourself financially, that distrust will echo in relationships. If you abandon yourself in love, that pattern will surface in business. If you overperform for success, you will likely overgive in intimacy. The thread underneath is always the same:

Safety

Worth

Self-trust

Coherence

When those stabilize internally, multiple areas begin to shift externally, sometimes faster than you expect.

How Alignment Looks in Real Life (Not Highlight Reels)

Alignment is quieter than people imagine. It does not look like constant breakthroughs or dramatic manifestations. It looks like responding instead of reacting. Choosing honesty over performance. Saying no without guilt. Pausing before forcing. Resting without explaining. Trusting yourself even when others don't understand.

Alignment feels less urgent. You stop asking, "Is this working?" every five minutes. You start asking, "Is this aligned?" And that question changes everything. Instead of chasing external validation, you check internal coherence. Instead of obsessing over timing, you evaluate congruence. Instead of trying to manage perception, you manage regulation.

This is not glamorous. It is powerful because alignment builds stability, and stability attracts sustainably.

A Story of When Things Finally Began to Move

There was a season when everything I wanted felt just out of reach.

Not gone. Just … delayed.

Money wasn't scarce, but it wasn't flowing with ease. Love was present, but not yet as deep and expansive as I knew it could be. Success was visible, but it felt like something I was performing rather than embodying. Old me would have panicked.

She would have doubled her effort. Forced more strategy. Overanalyzed conversations. Questioned her worth. Measured every delay as evidence of failure. But something was different. I trusted the process without stalling. I stayed engaged without gripping. I continued showing up, but I stopped strangling outcomes.

And then, almost imperceptibly at first, things began to click. Not dramatically. Not all at once.

But steadily. Opportunities that felt aligned instead of draining. Conversations that opened doors without pressure. Decisions that felt clean instead of anxious.

The shift wasn't external. It was internal.

I wasn't bracing anymore. Because of that, the external could reorganize naturally.

Recognizing Momentum Without Needing Proof

One of the most advanced skills in manifestation is recognizing momentum before visible results appear. If you wait for proof, you remain dependent on outcomes. If you can recognize internal momentum, you stabilize earlier.

Momentum shows up as:

Increased self-trust.

Decreased urgency.

Better discernment.

Faster emotional recovery.

Cleaner decisions.

These are not small things. They are evidence that your internal architecture has changed. And internal architecture determines what you can sustain. You may not yet see the financial breakthrough. But you notice you're no longer panicking when expenses arise.

You may not yet see the relationship shift. But you notice you're no longer abandoning yourself to keep the peace. You may not yet see the career expansion. But you notice you're no longer shrinking to avoid judgment.

That is momentum.

Manifestation doesn't end when you receive what you asked for. That's when integration begins.

Money arrives, and your system quietly asks, "Is this safe to keep?"

Love deepens, and your body asks, "Can I stay open without losing myself?"

Success expands, and your nervous system asks, "Can I hold this without burning out?"

This is why embodiment matters more than attraction. What you cannot hold, you cannot keep. It is not uncommon for someone to manifest more income and then unconsciously overspend, overcommit, or self-sabotage. It's not because they are flawed but because their nervous system has not yet integrated the new level.

Grounding practices become essential here. It's not to stay humble, but to stay regulated: Celebrating without inflating ego. Receiving without guilt. Continuing your rituals. Maintaining boundaries. Staying connected to your body as your world expands. Integration is not glamorous. It is stabilizing.

Staying Rooted While Expanding

Expansion without grounding creates anxiety. Grounding without expansion creates stagnation. The work is balance. You expand your capacity while staying rooted in your body, your values, and your nervous system.

This looks like:

Celebrating wins without becoming addicted to applause.

Receiving money without tightening around it.

Allowing love without abandoning independence.

Growing visibility without overexposing yourself.

Adjusting without collapsing.

It's not flashy. It's sustainable. Sustainability is the mark of mature manifestation. When money, love, and success begin talking to each other, what you are witnessing is not luck. It is integration. Your nervous system is no longer treating expansion as threat. Your identity is no longer splitting across domains. You are coherent. And coherence creates inevitability.

THE QUIET CONVERGENCE

There comes a point where you stop chasing separate goals and start noticing convergence. The same boundaries that improved your relationships strengthen your finances. The same self-trust that stabilized your love life improves your leadership. The same nervous system regulation that helped you receive money allows you to hold success.

This is not about juggling three different desires. It is about stabilizing one internal state.

Safety.

Clarity.

Self-trust.

Coherence.

When those align, money feels cleaner. Love feels steadier. Success feels lighter. You stop living in compartments. You live in integration.

And that is where manifestation becomes less about getting more and becomes more about being stable enough to sustain it. Not dramatic. Not chaotic. Coherent. And coherence changes everything.

WHEN OLD PATTERNS TRY TO RETURN

Even after alignment, old patterns may knock. Not because you failed. Not because you "lost" your manifestation. Not because the work didn't stick.

They return because familiarity is seductive.

Your nervous system is wired for what it knows. Even when what it knows is smaller, louder, or more chaotic than what you're building. Expansion is new. Regulation is new. Coherence is new. And the body will occasionally reach back for the familiar simply because it recognizes it.

You might feel the following urges:

Overwork when things start flowing.

Overgive when love feels stable.

Overexplain when success makes you visible.

Undercharge when money increases.

Settle when intimacy deepens.

Rush when patience would serve you better.

These impulses don't mean you are regressing. They mean you are integrating. Old patterns resurface at the edge of growth. They whisper, "This is unfamiliar. Let's go back to what we know." And what we know is often rooted in survival, not alignment.

This is where awareness saves you. You notice the urge. You feel the tightening.

You recognize the old story rising.

And instead of reacting, you pause.

That pause is power.

Because in that pause, you choose who you are becoming instead of who you used to be. Integration is not about never feeling triggered again. It's about responding differently when you are.

A Practice of Integration Over Acceleration

One of the most mature decisions you can make is choosing integration over acceleration. We live in a culture obsessed with speed. Faster growth. Faster money. Faster love. Faster impact. But not everything needs to move faster. Some things need to land deeper. When money expands, your nervous system needs time to recalibrate. When love deepens, your body needs time to learn safety. When success grows, your identity needs time to stabilize.

Without integration, even beautiful manifestations can feel overwhelming. You may manifest more income and suddenly feel anxious about keeping it. You may find secure love and feel the urge to create drama. You may achieve success and feel pressure to outperform your previous self.

Nothing is wrong. Your system is catching up. So, if things slow down, don't assume something broke. Ask a different question: "What is integrating right now?"

That question keeps you present instead of panicked. Integration is when your new identity becomes normal. What once felt like expansion becomes your baseline. You no longer flinch at abundance. You no longer brace for love to disappear. Success no longer feels like a performance. Acceleration builds momentum. Integration builds stability. And stability is what allows you to sustain what you've called in.

LETTING GO OF COMPARISON

Comparison dissolves when alignment strengthens. Comparison is not actually about other people. It is about uncertainty within yourself. It is the mind's attempt to measure safety through proximity to someone else's timeline. But when you trust your timing, others' timelines stop triggering you.

You realize:

Their success does not threaten yours.

Their pace does not dictate yours.

Their path has nothing to do with your capacity.

Comparison thrives in dysregulation. It quiets in coherence. When your nervous system feels safe, you do not interpret someone else's expansion as evidence of your lack. You see it as a possibility. You understand that seasons differ. Cycles differ. Assignments differ. You are not behind. You are on your path. That realization is freedom.

There is a quiet confidence that comes when manifestation becomes embodied. You stop needing to announce every move. You stop needing to prove your worth. You stop needing constant reassurance that it's "working."

You trust your process. You trust your discernment. You trust that if something feels off, you'll know how to respond. That trust is magnetic. It doesn't scream. It stabilizes.

People feel it before you speak. Opportunities respond to it before you chase. Life organizes around it because your internal state is no longer chaotic. This is mastery. Not perfection. Not constant growth. Not nonstop success. Mastery is emotional steadiness. Identity coherence. Nervous system regulation. The ability to recover quickly. The ability to adjust without collapsing. It's quiet. And it's powerful.

A Final Practice: The Coherence Check

Whenever money, love, or success feel off, return to the Four Pillars.

Ask yourself:

What am I thinking about this?

What am I feeling in my body?

What identity is activated right now?

What action am I taking or avoiding?

Notice where there is misalignment. Maybe your thoughts say, "This is safe," but your body is tight. Maybe your identity is still anchored in scarcity while your income is expanding. Maybe your action is avoidance disguised as patience. Gently bring them into coherence.

Shift the thought.

Regulate the emotion.

Upgrade the identity.

Take one aligned action.

This is not dramatic work. It is daily work. This is the 24/7 Manifestation Method in motion.

Closing: You Are Already Becoming

I want to leave you with this truth: You are not manifesting from who you will be someday. You are manifesting from who you are becoming right now.

Every aligned choice matters.

Every pause matters.

Every honest desire matters.

Money, love, and success are not rewards for getting it right. They are reflections of coherence. And coherence is something you practice, not something you earn.

You do not need to rush.

You do not need to force.

You do not need to shrink your desires to feel spiritual.

You need to stay present.

Stay honest.

Stay engaged.

Life responds to that. And once you are coherent, life gets louder with its guidance. Not superstition. Signal. In the next chapter, we're going to talk about signs, synchronicities, and discernment, so you can listen clearly without outsourcing your power.

Reflection Questions

Take your time with these questions. Do not rush them. There is no performance here.

1. Which area feels most regulated right now: money, love, or success?
2. Which feels most charged?
3. What belief might still be asking for reassurance?
4. Where have you already seen evidence of internal alignment?
5. How would your life feel if you trusted your timing completely?

Write honestly. You are not grading yourself. You are witnessing yourself. Awareness alone accelerates integration.

CHAPTER 9

Overcoming Resistance and Self-sabotage

There is a moment that arrives for almost everyone walking a conscious growth path. It isn't dramatic. It doesn't look like collapse. It doesn't even feel like fear.

It looks like postponement.

You still believe in the dream. You still journal about it. You still tell your friends it's coming. You just keep moving it.

Next month.

After the kids are older.

When work slows down.

When you feel more confident.

When you have more clarity.

Because it sounds responsible, it rarely gets questioned. Here is the truth: When you keep rescheduling the dream, it is not a time issue. It is an identity issue. And that realization changes everything. Beneath postponement is something quieter and more biological. Your ability to receive is directly tied to your ability to regulate. Manifestation is not just desire plus action. It is desire plus nervous system safety.

If your body does not feel safe with more, more visibility, more money, more love, more responsibility, it will unconsciously find reasons to remain where you are. Even if where you are feels tight.

Even if it quietly hurts. Familiar discomfort often feels safer than unfamiliar expansion. This is why resistance is so misunderstood.

Most people interpret resistance as laziness, a lack of motivation, a character flaw. So, they try to overpower it with better planning, tighter schedules, more discipline, and harsher self-talk. But resistance does not dissolve under force because resistance is not the problem. It is the signal. It is your nervous system whispering, "This future requires a version of you that does not yet feel stable."

That does not mean you cannot have it. It means you cannot have it as who you currently are. And that is not a flaw. It is biology. Self-sabotage is not self-hatred. It is self-protection. You are not avoiding success because you don't want it. You are hesitating because part of you believes it will cost you something: safety, belonging, approval, rest, love.

The subconscious does not negotiate with dreams. It negotiates with survival.

So, when a goal threatens the old identity, the people-pleaser, the struggler, the invisible one, the dependable one, the "good enough" one, your system pushes back. Not maliciously. Protectively. And once you understand that, you stop shaming yourself. You start evolving.

In this chapter, we'll begin to bring this into the light. You'll learn how to recognize the specific ways your system protects you, how self-sabotage shows up in your thoughts, behaviors, and emotional patterns, and why it has felt so difficult to move forward, even when you know what you want.

More importantly, you'll begin to shift your relationship with it. Not by forcing change but by understanding what your system is trying to preserve and learning how to create safety in new ways. Because once your system no longer sees growth as a threat, it stops resisting it. And that is when real change becomes possible.

When It's Not Scheduling, It's Identity

This is where most people get stuck. They tell themselves it's a time problem.

"I just need to organize my schedule better."

"I'll start when life slows down."

"I need one more certification."

"I just need to feel more ready."

But readiness is not a feeling. It's an identity threshold. When you repeatedly move the same dream, it's rarely because you lack discipline. It's because your current identity can imagine the future but cannot yet inhabit it.

You can see the version of you who speaks up, earns more, loves more deeply, and leads boldly. You can picture her. You might even admire her. But becoming her would require releasing the familiar version of you. And that is where the system hesitates. Because stepping forward means letting go of who you've been, even if who you've been was built around coping, pleasing, surviving, or staying small. Painful familiarity often feels safer than unknown expansion.

This is why mediocrity doesn't feel like failure. It feels like comfort. Mediocrity is seductive not because it's fulfilling, but because it's predictable.

It whispers:

"At least you know how this goes."

"At least you won't be disappointed."

"At least you won't stand out."

"At least you won't risk losing anything."

It doesn't attack you. It soothes you. And that's precisely why it's dangerous. Because comfort masquerades as safety while quietly suffocating your potential. There comes a moment when your life becomes good enough. And that is often the most dangerous moment of all.

"Good" doesn't require courage.

"Good" doesn't demand reinvention.

"Good" lets you remain who you are.

But great asks more. Great asks for visibility. For responsibility. For self-trust. For emotional risk. For consistency without applause. So, resistance appears right when things start to matter. Not when the dream is abstract. But when it's close enough to disrupt the identity that you've mastered.

That's when people stall. Not because they don't want great, but because great requires becoming someone new.

A STORY OF ALMOST

I've watched people circle the same dream for years. Same desire. Same language. Same "almost." They weren't lazy. They weren't incapable. They weren't unclear.

They were loyal.

Loyal to an identity that had once kept them safe.

There was the woman who told me, quietly, "If I actually succeed, people will expect more from me." Underneath her ambition was exhaustion. Success, to her nervous system, meant pressure. Another said, "If I stop struggling, I won't know who I am." Struggle had become her proof of worth. Ease felt foreign. Almost irresponsible.

Another admitted, "If I go all in and fail, I won't be able to pretend it wasn't important." As long as she hovered in almost, she could protect her heart from the clean sting of truth. Those aren't excuses. They're truths.

And when truths are named, sabotage begins to lose its grip because resistance is not a verdict on your potential. It is a threshold. Resistance appears at the edge of identity expansion. Not before. Not after. At the edge. It's the doorway. And you don't break through a doorway by shaming yourself. You walk through it by becoming someone new. Blame will not move you forward. Shame tightens the nervous system. Pressure collapses creativity. Force increases internal conflict.

But curiosity creates space. When you ask, "What is this protecting?" or "What would success require me to release?" you shift from self-attack to self-understanding. And understanding is what makes change sustainable. Here is the question most people avoid: What will it cost me if I don't change? Not in 10 years. Now.

What does staying the same require you to tolerate?

What dreams have gone quiet?

What parts of you have learned to stay small?

Resistance doesn't just block the dream. It keeps you loyal to an old story. And stories, no matter how long you've carried them, can be rewritten.

YOU ARE NOT BROKEN; YOU ARE AT AN EDGE

If this chapter feels uncomfortably accurate, that's a good sign. It means you're not stuck. You're not incapable. You're not flawed. You are standing at an identity threshold.

And thresholds feel tense. You don't need more discipline. You don't need another productivity system. You don't need to tighten your schedule or shame yourself into momentum.

You need to understand what version of you is being asked to emerge. Because resistance rarely announces itself as fear. If it did, you would recognize it immediately and call it what it is. Instead, resistance disguises itself as logic. It sounds reasonable. Responsible. Mature.

"Now isn't the right time."

"I just need more clarity."

"I should wait until things settle."

"I'll start when I feel more confident."

"I don't want to rush this."

And because these sentences sound intelligent, they go unchallenged. This is why so many capable people believe they're being patient when they're actually being avoidant. Not intentionally. Not consciously. But systemically. The nervous system protects familiarity at all costs, even when familiarity is limiting.

Readiness is one of the most misunderstood concepts in personal growth. It is not a feeling. It is not confidence. It is not certainty. It is not motivation. Readiness is an identity shift. You do not feel ready and then act. You act, and readiness forms around that action.

Confidence is built after movement, not before it. Waiting to feel ready keeps people in perpetual preparation. Another book. Another certification. Another plan refinement. Another round of research. Learning is valuable. But endless preparation is often fear in disguise. The subconscious is clever. It will happily let you "work on yourself" indefinitely if it means you never have to risk being seen.

Self-sabotage is rarely dramatic. It is subtle. Polite. Reasonable. It looks like saying yes to draining obligations right before you need creative energy. Overcommitting when something important is approaching. Procrastinating only on the things that matter most. Numbing out just as momentum builds.

Notice the pattern. You get busy right before the thing you care about. That is not poor time management. That is protection. So, when sabotage shows up, do not ask, "What's wrong with me?" Ask instead: "What is my body trying to avoid feeling?"

Pause for 30 seconds.

What am I feeling right now?

Where do I feel it in my body?

What would help my body feel 10% safer?

Ten percent is enough. We are not aiming for perfect regulation. We are aiming for sufficient safety to stay in motion. You are not broken. You are at an edge. And edges are where becoming begins.

THE NERVOUS SYSTEM AND THE FEAR OF EXPANSION

Your nervous system has one primary job: keep you alive. It does not care about your dreams.

It does not care about your vision board. It does not care about your unrealized potential.

It cares about familiarity.

Familiar equals predictable. Predictable equals survivable. And survivable, to the nervous system, equals safe. So, when expansion threatens to move you beyond what is known, your system reacts. Not always with dramatic panic. Sometimes with fatigue. Sometimes with distraction. Sometimes with sudden doubt that feels strangely rational.

This is why people often feel tired right before a breakthrough. Why they procrastinate the very opportunity they've been praying for. Why they question themselves at the edge of visibility. It is not incapacity. It is recalibration. Expansion requires more capacity. More visibility. More responsibility. More choice. And choice can feel unsafe if you were raised to survive instead of thrive. If love felt conditional. If rest felt earned. If success felt risky.

The body does not differentiate between a lion in the grass and a leap in identity. It only registers unfamiliar territory. That sensation you label as fear is often just your system adjusting to a larger life.

FEAR IS NOT THE ENEMY

It's the threshold. Here is the reframe that changes everything: fear does not mean stop. Fear means edge. Fear shows up when you are about to be seen differently.

When you are about to leave an old identity behind.

When you are about to risk disappointment.

When you are about to claim authority.

If fear were a stop sign, no one would ever evolve. Fear is not a verdict. It is a threshold.

THE 90-SECOND RULE: DISARMING OVERWHELM IN REAL TIME

Emotion is not the enemy. Unprocessed emotion is. Most emotional waves crest quickly when allowed to move. Often, the intensity lasts about 90 seconds. The problem is not the wave. The problem is the story we attach to it. We replay. We catastrophize. We rehearse the worst. We turn a sensation into an identity.

The practice is simple:

Name it. "This is fear." "This is shame." "This is overwhelm."

Locate it in the body: chest, throat, belly, jaw.

Breathe and observe the sensation like weather moving through. No fixing. No narrative.

Stay with sensation for 90 seconds.

When the wave softens, choose one clean next step.

You do not argue with fear. You metabolize it. And in doing so, you teach your body that expansion is survivable.

When Anger Was Actually Grief

I once worked with a woman who described herself as "angry all the time." She was short with her partner. Irritable at work. Frustrated by small things. She believed anger was her problem.

As she moved through the 24/7 Manifestation Method, something else emerged. Underneath the anger was grief. She was carrying a grief that she never gave herself permission to feel. Grief from years of over-functioning. Grief from carrying responsibility without support. Grief from being strong for everyone else.

Anger had become the shield.

When she slowed down enough to feel the grief instead of fighting it, the anger softened almost immediately. Her nervous system didn't need the armor anymore. Her relationships changed.

Her communication softened. Her sense of ease returned.

Nothing external "fixed" her life. She simply stopped resisting the emotion that wanted to move. That is emotional alignment. And that alignment changed how life responded to her.

That's what regulation does. It turns emotion into information instead of sabotage.

EFT TAPPING: MOVING FEAR OUT OF THE BODY

Sometimes the wave doesn't move in 90 seconds because it's not today's fear. It's old fear. Stored fear. The kind your system learned a long time ago. This is where tapping is useful. Not as a magic trick but as a discharge tool.

Simple tapping sequence (two minutes):
Tap gently while saying the truth.

- "Even though I feel ___, I accept myself and I'm willing to feel safe."
- "Even though part of me wants to shrink, I'm choosing expansion."
- "Even though this feels unfamiliar, I can move anyway."

Tap through a few points (karate chop, eyebrow, side of eye, under eye, collarbone) and keep it simple: name the fear, name the desire, choose safety.

The goal is not to force confidence. The goal is to reduce charge so that aligned action is possible.

WHY COMFORT CAN BE MORE DANGEROUS THAN FAILURE

Failure gets a bad reputation. We treat it like a verdict on our intelligence, our worth, our capacity. But failure is loud. It gets your attention. It demands adjustment. It forces growth.

Comfort, on the other hand, is quiet.

Comfort whispers, *This is fine.*

Don't rock the boat.

At least you know how this goes.

Comfort doesn't wound you. It lulls you. And that's why it's dangerous. Comfort keeps you tolerating what no longer fits. It convinces you that stability is the same thing as safety. It persuades you to trade aliveness for predictability. Over time, the misalignment doesn't explode. It dulls. The edges of your ambition soften. The urgency fades. The dream becomes a polite idea instead of a living desire.

The longer you tolerate what no longer aligns, the more resistance grows. Not because you are failing, but because something in you knows you are meant for more. Risking good for great is one of the bravest decisions you will ever make because "good" gives you something to lose: A steady paycheck. A familiar relationship. A manageable routine. Walking away from dysfunction is easy. Walking away from adequacy requires courage.

Avoidance has a cost, and it is rarely immediate. It accumulates quietly. It costs self-trust. It costs momentum. It costs clarity. It costs aliveness.

Every time you postpone something that matters to you, your system records it. Not with punishment. With data. It learns: *I don't back myself. My desires aren't safe. Follow-through is optional.* Over time, this erodes confidence more deeply than failure ever could. Failure at least proves you were willing to try. Avoidance teaches you to doubt your own word.

INTERRUPTING THE PATTERN WITHOUT FORCE

You do not need to shame yourself into change. You do not need to bulldoze resistance. You need to interrupt the pattern gently but decisively. Instead of asking, *Why am I like this?*

Ask, *What would the version of me who trusts herself do next?*

Not the entire plan. Not the dramatic leap. Just the next clean step. Resistance weakens in the presence of movement. Not dramatic movement. Consistent movement.

NEVER LEAVE A DECISION WITHOUT A COMMITMENT

A decision without a commitment is a wish. When you decide, anchor it in behavior.

"I want to write the book" becomes "I will write for 20 minutes tomorrow morning."

"I want to prioritize my health" becomes "I will walk for 10 minutes today."

Commitment grounds intention into the body. Without it, your nervous system reopens the loop and negotiates its way back to comfort. And comfort, left unexamined, will always choose the familiar over the extraordinary.

MOMENTUM IS BUILT, NOT FOUND

Momentum is not a mood that descends on you one lucky morning. It is not inspiration striking like lightning. It is not confidence finally arriving to escort you forward. Momentum is built. It is created through motion. And motion does not require certainty. It requires willingness.

One small step creates energy. Energy creates clarity. Clarity creates confidence.

Most people reverse the order. They wait to feel confident before they act. They wait to feel clear before they begin. They wait to feel fearless before they move. But confidence is a byproduct, not a prerequisite. This is why action is the cure for fear.

Not frantic action. Not performative action. Not the kind fueled by panic. Aligned action. The kind that says, *I am willing to move even while I am unsure.* Willingness is quiet. It does not demand guarantees. It does not negotiate with perfection. It simply moves.

A STORY OF CHOOSING MOVEMENT

I once worked with a woman who had been "almost ready" for years. She had the credentials. The experience. The network. The resources. On paper, she was overqualified for the life she said she wanted.

But she was waiting.

Waiting to feel certain. Waiting to feel more prepared. Waiting for the invisible moment when everything would align and fear would disappear. The shift came when she stopped asking, "Am I ready?" And started asking, "Am I willing?"

Willing to be uncomfortable.

Willing to be visible.

Willing to risk being imperfect.

That one shift changed the trajectory of her life. Not because it eliminated fear, but because it ended the negotiation with it. She moved while afraid. She applied before she felt polished. She spoke before she felt invincible. The results did not appear overnight. But something more powerful happened. She became someone who followed through. And that identity created results she could sustain.

REFRAMING FAILURE

Failure is not a stop sign. It is a qualifier.

It asks:

Do you want this enough to adjust?

Can you stay present when it's messy?

Are you committed to growth, not just applause?

Every person you admire has failed publicly, privately, painfully. What separates them is not talent. It is resilience. They did not interpret discomfort as a verdict. They interpreted it as refinement. Failure does not destroy identity. Quitting does.

THE IDENTITY SHIFT THAT ENDS SELF-SABOTAGE

Self-sabotage dissolves when identity shifts. You stop seeing yourself as someone who tries and start seeing yourself as someone who participates. Identity is not built through affirmations. It is built through evidence. Small behaviors, repeated consistently, teach your nervous system that it is safe to expand.

When your actions say, *I follow through*, your system begins to believe it.

MOVING WITH RESISTANCE

You do not need to eliminate resistance. You need to move with it. Like a current in water, resistance cannot be defeated through force. When you fight it, you exhaust yourself. When you avoid it, you drift backward. When you move with awareness, it carries you forward.

Right before a breakthrough, fear often gets louder. Irritability rises. Doubt surfaces. Unexpected obstacles appear. This is not punishment. It is proximity. When the old identity senses it is about to be replaced, it protests. Not because you are off track, but because you are close.

Discomfort is not a red light. It is a threshold. You do not sabotage what does not matter to you. You sabotage what threatens to change you. Once you understand that, the fight dissolves. You stop trying to destroy resistance. And you start becoming someone bigger than it.

This is how to cross the threshold:

1. **Normalize the fear**
   When fear shows up, don't spiral. Speak to it: "I see you. I hear you. But I'm not shrinking this time. I'm expanding."
2. **Do the opposite of what fear wants**
   Fear wants you quiet, small, invisible, or stuck. So, take micro-aligned action: hit publish; send the email; ask the question; raise the rate; set the boundary.
3. **Regulate first, then move**
   Use 4-7-8 breathing, the 90-second rule, or tapping. You're not trying to be fearless. You're trying to be steady.
4. **Journal or script through it**
   Ask: "What are you afraid will happen?" Then reframe: "Even if the worst happens, I will still be okay. And what if it goes better than I imagined?"
5. **Anchor into the future you**
   Close your eyes. Drop into the version of you who already has it. Ask: "What would you do right now?" Then do that.

When the Nudge Comes, Move

There was a moment at one of my retreats that perfectly illustrated this principle.

At the beginning of each Journey retreat, I invite every woman to bring a small gift. Nothing extravagant. Just something meaningful. We place the gifts in the center, and each woman draws a number at random. It's one of my favorite rituals because it allows the universe to rearrange things without us interfering.

That year, I had brought an oracle deck.

As the women reached into the coconut bowl to draw their numbers, a young woman named Amina softly introduced herself. Her voice was barely above a whisper. Even as she spoke, I could feel the hesitancy in her body. Not insecurity exactly. More like untapped power waiting for permission.

In that moment, I heard a quiet internal nudge: If she pulls your number, give her access to SpeakHer.

SpeakHer was a live program happening two days after the retreat. A space for women to build confidence, own their voice, and eventually step onto a stage. It wasn't a small gift. It wasn't something I had planned to offer.

My mind immediately tried to negotiate.

That's impulsive.

You didn't budget for that.

What if she doesn't use it?

What if you're overextending?

This is what I've learned about resistance. When fear speaks loudly, guidance usually whispers. And you must decide which voice you're loyal to. Amina reached into the bowl. She pulled my number. The oracle deck was hers. And without overthinking, without opening the door to debate, I followed through. I told her she would also receive full access to SpeakHer.

She looked stunned. Then excited. Then emotional. What I didn't know at the time was that she lived only a few hours from where the event would be held. The logistics were easy. The timing aligned. The door was open. If I had paused to analyze it, I might have talked myself out of it. If I had waited to feel certain, the moment would have passed. That's how resistance works. It doesn't always tell you to shrink. Sometimes it tells you to stall.

Micro-aligned action is not always dramatic. It's clean. You feel the nudge. You check that it's aligned. You move.

No spiraling.

No over-explaining.

No bargaining with fear.

This is what it means to do the opposite of what fear wants. Fear wants you to hesitate.

Fear wants you to rationalize. Fear wants you to keep things contained and predictable. But expansion often arrives disguised as a quiet instruction. And the more quickly you act on aligned nudges, the more your nervous system learns:

I can trust myself.

I respond.

I don't freeze when something matters.

That is how identity shifts. Not through declarations. Through clean decisions. When guidance comes, act cleanly. Don't overthink it.

The Real Opponent Was Never Fear; It Was Loyalty to the Old Self.

Most people believe they're afraid of failure. But if you look closely, that's rarely the full story. What they are actually afraid of is success without the old narrative that defined them.

Who are you without struggle?

Who are you without chaos to manage?

Who are you without constantly proving your worth?

Who are you if you are no longer the strong one, the fixer, the overachiever, the one who survives impossible things?

The old identity may be tired. It may be heavy. It may even be painful. But it is familiar. And familiarity feels like safety to the nervous system. So, when resistance appears, it is not a betrayal of your dream. It is loyalty to the version of you that once kept you safe:

The overworker who earned love through performance.

The people-pleaser who avoided conflict to maintain belonging.

The struggler who felt worthy only when overcoming something hard.

If success threatens to remove those roles, the system hesitates. Not because you are incapable. Because you are evolving.

When you understand this, the shame dissolves. You stop asking, "Why am I like this?" and start asking, "Who am I loyal to?" And then the work shifts. You are no longer fighting fear. You are renegotiating identity.

Identity Is Built Through Evidence, Not Affirmations

You cannot think your way into a new identity.

You can declare, "I am confident."

You can repeat, "I am disciplined."

You can insist, "I am someone who follows through."

But if your behavior contradicts those declarations, your nervous system does not believe you. The body believes evidence. Identity is not installed through language. It is installed through repetition. If you want to become someone who follows through, you follow through on something small. If you want to become someone who is courageous, you take one courageous action before you feel ready. If you want to become someone who trusts herself, you keep one promise you made to yourself.

Small behaviors. Repeated consistently. That is how identity changes without force.

This is why self-sabotage dissolves through practice, not pressure. Not through affirmations shouted over doubt, but through evidence accumulated over time.

Becoming the Person Who Doesn't Negotiate with Herself

There is a quiet power in becoming someone who does not negotiate with her own commitments. Not rigidly. Not harshly. But cleanly.

"If I say I'll do something, I do it."

"If I choose something, I honor it."

"If I change my mind, I do it consciously, not reactively."

This is not about perfection. It is about integrity. When you stop negotiating with yourself, your nervous system relaxes. It no longer has to question whether your decisions are temporary or conditional. It learns that your word matters. Self-trust builds in these micro-moments.

And self-trust dissolves sabotage faster than motivation ever could. Because once you trust yourself, resistance loses its leverage.

The Shift from Trying to Being

Trying is unstable. Being is grounded. Trying says, "I hope I follow through." Being says, "This is who I am." Trying waits for the right mood. Being acts regardless of mood. Trying negotiates. Being commits. The shift from trying to being is subtle but profound. You do not announce it. You embody it.

You write even when it feels inconvenient.

You speak even when your voice shakes.

You rest without apology.

You choose alignment over relief.

Congruence replaces chaos. And congruence is magnetic.

Your self-concept is not a personality trait. It is a pattern:

A pattern of how you speak to yourself.

A pattern of how you respond to discomfort.

A pattern of how you treat your promises.

And patterns can be redesigned. Not through willpower alone, but through structure.

You reduce friction.

You create environments that support follow-through.

You set commitments that are realistic enough to honor.

You choose consistency over intensity.

This is not weakness. It is wisdom. When your life supports your nervous system, resistance softens naturally.

The Moment You Choose Yourself

There is always a defining moment. It rarely looks dramatic. There are no fireworks. No applause. It happens quietly.

When you do the thing even though you don't feel like it.

When you tell the truth instead of managing perception.

When you choose the long game over immediate comfort.

When you stay present instead of numbing.

When you act in alignment, even without recognition.

In that moment, something rewires. Your system registers: *I can trust myself.* And once that registration happens, everything changes. Because the real opponent was never fear. It was the outdated identity you were protecting. And now, you are no longer protecting it. You are becoming someone new.

As your identity begins to shift, something subtle but unmistakable happens. Old patterns stop feeling tempting. They start feeling uncomfortable.

Procrastination no longer feels like relief. It feels heavy. Avoidance no longer feels protective. It feels dishonest. Excuses that once sounded convincing now echo hollow.

You don't outgrow sabotage because you've become stricter with yourself.

You outgrow it because you've become clearer.

Clarity changes your tolerance. When you can see the pattern, you can't unsee it. The late-night numbing, the last-minute cancellations, the self-deprecating jokes, the strategic shrinking. They no longer feel like personality traits. They feel like outdated strategies.

And outdated strategies eventually chafe. This is not hardness. It's coherence. When who you are becoming is stronger than who you were protecting, sabotage loses its seduction.

The Courage to Risk Being Seen as New

One of the final layers of resistance is not internal. It's relational.

What will people think when you change?

When you stop over-explaining?

When you stop apologizing for your needs?

When you no longer play the role they've grown comfortable with?

Growth disrupts dynamics. The dependable one becomes discerning. The quiet one becomes vocal. The accommodating one develops boundaries. And not everyone will know what to do with that. This is where many people retreat. Not because they doubt themselves, but because they fear relational loss.

But here is the deeper truth: the people who truly belong in your future will adjust to your expansion. They may need time. They may need recalibration. But they will not require you to shrink to remain. Risking good for great includes risking outdated roles.

That isn't betrayal. It's evolution.

The New Relationship with Failure

At this stage, failure loses its sting. Not because you enjoy it. But because you understand it. Failure does not undo identity. Quitting does.

Failure refines you. Quitting fragments you.

When you fail and continue, your nervous system learns resilience. When you avoid entirely, it learns hesitation. So, you stop fearing mistakes. You begin fearing stagnation more. And that shift alone changes your trajectory.

Living as Someone Who Follows Through

Following through is not a personality trait. It's a practice. A practice of choosing alignment over comfort. Integrity over avoidance. Growth over familiarity.

You don't wait to feel different. You act differently, and the feeling catches up. Identity is not declared. It is installed.

I've watched people who once insisted they were inconsistent become profoundly reliable.

Not through force. Not through pressure.

But through honesty. They stopped making promises they weren't ready to keep. And they started keeping the ones they made.

Not more promises. Cleaner ones. Not bigger goals. Truer ones.

That is the quiet shift. And that is how self-sabotage dissolves—not dramatically, but permanently.

Practice: Identity Installation

Take a moment with your journal.

Complete these sentences honestly:

- "The version of me I'm outgrowing is ..."
- "The version of me I'm becoming values ..."
- "One behavior that proves my new identity is ..."
- "One promise I will keep this week is ..."

Then keep it. That's the work.

When Alignment Feels Uncomfortable (And Why That's a Good Sign)

One of the most confusing moments for people new to intentional manifestation is this: things can feel *worse* before they feel better. Not worse in a catastrophic way, but uncomfortable in a revealing way. You might feel restless. Irritable. Emotionally tender. More aware of what no longer fits.

This is not a sign that something is wrong. It's a sign that something is **coming into focus**.

When you begin interrupting old habit loops and installing new ones, the subconscious often responds by surfacing what has been running quietly underneath the surface. Patterns that once operated invisibly now become obvious. Thoughts you used to accept automatically suddenly feel heavy or false. Situations you once tolerated begin to feel loud. That discomfort is not punishment. It's information.

It's the nervous system recalibrating. It's identity reorganizing. It's awareness expanding.

Most people quit here. Not because they are incapable, but because they misinterpret discomfort as failure instead of initiation.

Closing: You Are No Longer Negotiating with Your Potential

Here is what I want you to know as you close this chapter: You are not someone who self-sabotages. You are someone who has been protecting an outdated identity. And now, you're ready to release it.

Not through force.

Not through shame.

But through embodiment.

You don't need to become someone else. You need to **become consistent with who you are already becoming**. Resistance no longer controls you. It informs you.

And self-trust replaces self-sabotage, not overnight, but permanently.

In the next chapter, we will move into recognizing signs, synchronicities, and guidance without outsourcing your authority. Not magical thinking. Discernment.

Because once resistance no longer runs the show, clarity sharpens. And life starts responding in unmistakable ways. You're not imagining it. You're finally aligned.

Reflection Questions

Sit with these questions:

1. Where have I been loyal to an identity that no longer fits?
2. What does resistance protect me from losing?
3. Where am I ready to risk good for great?
4. What small action would reinforce my new self-concept today?
5. What would change if I trusted myself completely?

Write without judgment. This is integration.

CHAPTER 10

Living in Overflow: Default Mode Manifestation

There is a quiet myth that sits at the center of most manifestation teachings. The myth is that one day, you *arrive*. That there will be a moment where the work is done and the habits are locked in. The fears are gone. The manifestations stack neatly on top of each other. And from that moment forward, life is smooth.

Overflowing. Effortless. Solved.

But that isn't how real lives work. And if you've made it this far in this book, something in you already knows that.

Overflow is not a destination. It is a **way of living**. And living in overflow doesn't mean life stops presenting challenges. It means **you meet life differently because you are different**.

For years, I believed that once I manifested "enough," I would finally exhale.

Enough money.

Enough security.

Enough clarity.

Enough success.

I thought overflow would feel like completion. Instead, what I discovered was something far more honest. Life didn't stop asking things of me. But I stopped collapsing under the asking.

That's the difference.

When people talk about "having it all," what they're usually describing is not a perfect life. They're describing **capacity**. The capacity to hold complexity without panic. The capacity to move through discomfort without self-betrayal. The capacity to expand without losing themselves. Overflow is not about what you have.

It's about **what you can hold**.

Default Mode Manifestation

Up until now, much of this book has focused on conscious practice.

Intentional thought.

Emotional regulation.

Identity shifting.

Aligned action.

Surrender without stalling.

Releasing sabotage.

All of that matters. But at some point, manifestation stops being something you actively manage. It becomes your **default mode**. Not because you're trying harder. But because you've rehearsed a new way of being so consistently that it runs automatically.

Default mode manifestation means

- your nervous system expects support instead of threat;
- your mind looks for possibilities instead of problems;
- your body recovers faster from stress;
- your identity no longer negotiates with old limits.

You don't manifest *occasionally*. You manifest **continuously** because you are always broadcasting from a regulated, coherent state.

That's overflow.

One of the most important mindset shifts that allows overflow to stabilize is this: **you choose growth over arrival**.

Arrival is static. Growth is alive.

When you orient your life around arrival, you become fragile. Every setback feels personal.

Every delay feels like failure. Every challenge feels like proof that something isn't working. But when you orient around growth, life stays dynamic. Challenges don't disappear. They evolve. And so do you.

Overflow doesn't mean you stop growing. It means growth stops feeling like a threat. You stop asking, "When will this be over?" And start asking, "Who am I becoming through this?"

Why Life Feels Different Now

People often say, "My life feels different since I started this work." What they usually mean is not that circumstances changed overnight. It's that **their internal experience changed first**.

They don't spiral the same way. They don't catastrophize as quickly. They don't abandon themselves under pressure. They don't confuse discomfort with danger.

Life feels different because **you are different**. This is one of the most overlooked markers of real manifestation. External results lag behind internal shifts. Always.

So, if things feel calmer, clearer, or more grounded even before the "big manifestations" arrive, that's not a consolation prize. That's evidence.

Your life is not shaped by what you want occasionally. It is shaped by what you **rehearse daily**.

You rehearse:

- How you talk to yourself when things go wrong
- How quickly you assume blame or trust
- How you respond to uncertainty
- How you treat your own needs
- How you recover from disappointment

These rehearsals become habits. Habits become identity. Identity becomes reality. Overflow is not created by one breakthrough moment. It's created by **consistent internal rehearsal**. This is why people can "manifest" something once and then lose it. They attracted it consciously but couldn't *hold it unconsciously*. Default mode manifestation means your unconscious is finally on board.

Progress Over Perfection

Let's dismantle another dangerous idea. That overflow means you get it "right" all the time. It doesn't. Overflow lives in **progress, not perfection**.

Perfection is rigid.

Progress is adaptive.

Perfection collapses under pressure.

Progress adjusts.

When you live in overflow, you

- notice misalignment faster,
- repair more quickly,
- apologize sooner,
- recalibrate without drama, and
- keep moving without self-attack.

This is not spiritual bypassing. This is emotional maturity. Your nervous system no longer treats imperfection as a threat to belonging. And that frees up enormous energy.

Your Capacity Grow

This is one of the most grounding truths of overflow. Problems don't vanish.

Your **capacity expands**.

What once felt overwhelming now feels manageable. What once triggered panic now triggers curiosity. What once stopped you now slows you briefly. This is not because life got easier. It's because you got stronger in the ways that matter. Overflow doesn't mean a problem-free life.

It means a **resilient self**. And resilience is magnetic.

There was a time when one unexpected bill would send my entire system into survival mode. My chest would tighten. My mind would spiral. My sense of safety would collapse.

Years later, the numbers are larger. The responsibilities are greater. The stakes are higher.

And yet … my body is calmer. It's not because nothing goes wrong. But because I trust myself to respond. That trust is overflow.

Not abundance as a number. Abundance as **self-reliance without isolation**.

Overflow Is Not Constant High Vibration

This is critical to say clearly. Living in overflow does not mean you are happy all the time. Or calm all the time. Or grateful all the time.

That expectation creates spiritual exhaustion. Overflow is grounded.

It includes

- grief without collapse,
- anger without destruction,
- fear without paralysis, and
- joy without clinging.

You experience the full range of being human. But you no longer live at the mercy of your emotions. You move *with* them.

That's regulation. That's maturity. That's mastery.

Earlier in the journey, personal growth often feels like fixing.

Fixing thoughts. Fixing patterns. Fixing habits. Fixing wounds.

But overflow begins when you stop living as a project. You're not constantly correcting yourself. You're **inhabiting yourself**. Growth becomes integrated instead of effortful. You don't wake up asking, "What do I need to work on today?" You wake up asking, "How do I want to live today?"

Many people are surprised that overflow doesn't arrive loudly. It arrives quietly.

As steadiness. As discernment. As choice. As self-respect.

You realize you're no longer tolerating what drains you. You're no longer chasing what destabilizes you. You're no longer performing for approval. Your life simplifies.

And simplicity creates space. Space is where overflow actually lives.

Here's a simple way to recognize default mode manifestation forming:

Ask yourself:

- How do I respond when things don't go my way?
- How quickly do I recover?

- How much do I trust myself to handle what comes next?
- How often do I abandon myself under stress?

Your answers reveal more than any manifestation journal ever could.

If you take nothing else from this section, take this: Overflow is not a peak experience.

It is a **baseline state**.

A baseline of self-trust. A baseline of regulation. A baseline of responsiveness instead of reactivity.

Let's go deeper:

- Overflow changes your relationship with time, money, and effort.
- Why is ease often misinterpreted as laziness?
- How can you live in expansion without burnout?
- Default mode manifestation reshapes your identity long term.

This is where the work stops being something you *do* and becomes something you *live*. One of the most disorienting moments in this work is realizing that ease can feel unfamiliar. Not suspicious in a dramatic way. Just … quiet.

No adrenaline. No urgency. No chaos demanding your attention. And for many people, that quiet is uncomfortable. Not because something is wrong. But because their nervous system has been trained to associate intensity with aliveness.

So, when overflow begins to stabilize, the mind asks:

"Shouldn't this feel bigger?"

"Why am I not more excited?"

"Am I doing enough?"

This is where people often unconsciously recreate struggle. Not because they want pain.

But because they don't yet trust peace.

OVERFLOW IS A LIFESTYLE

Overflow isn't a moment you earn. It's a baseline you build. It's what happens when your nervous system stops treating life as a threat and starts treating life as something you can meet. That's why the real goal isn't one manifestation. It's stability. Because when stability becomes your default, you stop trying to "get lucky" with abundance and start living as someone who can hold it. In Part 2, we'll install the three stabilizers that keep your magnet charged: emotional regulation, environmental design, and spiritual practices that clear your field without making your life a full-time self-improvement project.

When Decluttering Changed Everything

There was a woman named Nisha who came into this work feeling stagnant. Not depressed.

Not hopeless. Just … flat. She described her life as passionless. Like she was moving through her days without spark or momentum. She wanted desire back. Aliveness. Direction.

As she worked through the 24/7 Manifestation Method, she noticed something unexpected: her environment started to feel loud. Her home was filled with unfinished projects. Items she meant to fix. Clothes she didn't wear. Objects carrying the weight of "someday." And suddenly, a rule came to her with absolute clarity: "If it hasn't been fixed in a year, it's not mine to fix."

So, she started letting things go.

Box by box. Drawer by drawer. Promise by promise.

What she was really releasing wasn't clutter. It was stagnant energy. Deferred decisions. Old identities.

She was changing the **energetic architecture** of her life. Within days, her mood lifted.

Her energy returned. Her actions became consistent. Nothing "external" had happened yet. But internally, she had made space. And when space is made, life rushes in to fill it.

Passion didn't arrive as a lightning bolt. It returned as momentum. That's manifestation through alignment.

THE THREE STABILIZERS OF OVERFLOW

If manifestation is a magnet, overflow is not the moment you "get the thing." Overflow is the magnet staying charged on an average Tuesday.

Most people can access a high vibe moment: A good meditation. A powerful retreat breakthrough. A journaling session that cracks them open. But default mode manifestation is different. It is what you can sustain. It is what your nervous system can hold without spiraling, gripping, or self-abandoning when life gets messy.

This is why overflow is not maintained through intensity. It is maintained through stability. And stability is built through three stabilizers. Think of them as the supports that keep your energy clear, grounded, and powerful without requiring you to be perfect.

STABILIZER ONE: EMOTIONAL REGULATION

Emotional regulation is your ability to return to safety quickly. Not to positivity. Not to performance. Safety.

When your nervous system is regulated, you stop treating discomfort like danger. You can feel disappointment without collapsing. You can feel fear without freezing. You can feel desire without clinging. Regulation is what makes receiving possible, because your body stops interpreting "more" as a threat.

A simple way to work with this is what I call the 10% return.

When you notice yourself slipping into overwhelm, ask:

- What am I feeling right now?
- Where do I feel it in my body?
- What would help me feel 10% safer?

Ten percent is enough to keep moving. Ten percent is enough to stop the spiral from becoming a story. Ten percent is how you teach your body that expansion is survivable. This is how overflow becomes your baseline. Not because life stops happening, but because you stop leaving yourself when it does.

STABILIZER TWO: ENVIRONMENTAL DESIGN

Your environment is either reinforcing your overflow or draining it. A lot of people try to manifest abundance while living inside energetic static. Cluttered spaces. Unfinished projects. Endless small reminders of what they have not completed. Constant friction and decision fatigue.

Your space is not just physical. It is psychological. Your home, your schedule, your notifications, your relationships, your calendar. All of it broadcasts instructions to your nervous system.

Environmental design is the art of making your life easier to live in. Not because you are lazy, but because you are done suffering for your goals.

Here is a simple environmental audit. Write down your answers without judgment:

1. What is quietly draining me every day that I have normalized?
2. What am I tolerating that I could simplify, automate, or release?
3. What unfinished item keeps pulling on my attention like a loose thread?
4. Where am I making everything harder than it needs to be?

Overflow is not built by adding more. It is built by removing what taxes your system. This is why decluttering can be a spiritual practice. Because when you change your environment, you change what your nervous system expects. And what your nervous system expects becomes your baseline.

STABILIZER THREE: SPIRITUAL HYGIENE

Spiritual hygiene is how you keep your field clear, grounded, and connected. Not performative. Not complicated. Not another thing to "do right." Think of spiritual hygiene the same way you think about brushing your teeth. You do not brush your teeth once and declare yourself done forever. You do it because maintenance is love.

Spiritual hygiene can be simple:

- A two-minute grounding practice in the morning with your feet on the floor, hand on heart, breath moving slowly.
- A quick "return to self" reset between meetings, hand on belly, one deep exhale, and the reminder: I am here. I am safe. I am guided.
- A nightly energy rinse in the shower, imagining the day washing off your body, releasing what is not yours to carry.
- A short prayer or altar moment that is not about asking for outcomes, but about remembering connection.

You do not need to be constantly high vibration. You need to be in relationship with your energy. The most powerful people are not the people who never get shaken. They are the people who know how to come back.

WHY THESE THREE STABILIZERS MATTER

Most people think manifestation is about wanting something and thinking positively until it arrives. But overflow requires something deeper. It requires nervous system safety. It requires a life designed for coherence. It requires practices that bring you back to yourself again and again.

When these three stabilizers are in place, you stop living in a cycle of peaks and crashes. You stop "finding" alignment and then losing it. You stop manifesting in bursts and then burning out. You begin to live in a steadier frequency. Not because nothing challenges you, but because your foundation holds. And once your foundation holds, your magnet stays charged. That is default mode manifestation.

When Ease Feels Like Laziness

Let's talk about one of the most deeply conditioned beliefs in our culture: If it's not hard, it must not be valuable. Many people have internalized the idea that effort equals worth. That rest must be earned. That ease must be justified. That success must cost something. So, when default mode manifestation begins to take hold and life feels more spacious, the old conditioning flares up.

"You should be doing more."

"Don't get complacent."

"This can't last."

"If you slow down, you'll lose momentum."

These thoughts don't mean you're regressing. They mean you're shedding a survival-based relationship with effort. Overflow does not remove effort from life. It removes **strain**.

The Difference Between Effort and Strain

Effort is clean. Strain is exhausting.

Effort comes from clarity. Strain comes from fear.

Effort says, "I'm choosing this."

Strain says, "I'm afraid of what happens if I don't."

When you live in overflow, you still work. You still show up. You still stretch. But you are no longer fighting yourself while you do it. That internal war dissolves. And when it does, energy returns. Not in bursts. In consistency.

How Overflow Changes Your Relationship with Time

One of the first things people notice when default mode manifestation stabilizes is that time feels different. Not because there's more of it. But because there's less resistance to it.

You stop racing the clock. You stop trying to "catch up." You stop feeling behind as a baseline state. This happens because urgency loosens its grip. Urgency is a survival response. Overflow is a regulated state. When urgency fades, presence increases. You become more responsive instead of reactive. And responsiveness is where intelligent action lives.

Living Without the Constant Internal Deadline

Many people live with an invisible internal deadline.

"I should be further by now."

"I'm running out of time."

"I'm behind everyone else."

This internal pressure drains more energy than any external demand. Overflow does not erase ambition. It removes self-threat.

You still want things. You still move toward them. But you're no longer punishing yourself along the way. And that changes the quality of your actions. They become clearer. Cleaner. More effective.

Why Progress Matters More Than Pace

In survival mode, speed feels important. Faster feels safer. More feels better. Busy feels productive.

In overflow, **progress** matters more than pace. You understand that slow, consistent movement compounds. You trust the process enough to let things unfold organically. You stop equating frantic action with success. This is not passivity. It's discernment.

You act when it's aligned. You pause when it's not. And you don't make either mean something about your worth.

Problems Don't Disappear, Your Capacity Grows

This truth becomes especially clear here. Life does not suddenly stop presenting challenges. But your relationship to them changes. What once felt like a crisis now feels like a problem to solve. What once sent you spiraling now invites curiosity. What once felt personal now feels contextual. This is not because you've hardened. It's because you've expanded.

Your nervous system can hold more complexity without collapse. That's overflow. Not the absence of problems. The presence of capacity.

A Story of Capacity Over Circumstances

I remember a moment where several things went wrong at once. A schedule shift. A financial curveball. An emotional conversation I hadn't anticipated. Years earlier, this combination would have flattened me.

I would have gone into fix-it mode. Or blame. Or self-attack.

This time, something else happened. I paused. I breathed. I responded one piece at a time. Not perfectly. But steadily. That's when I realized something had fundamentally changed. My circumstances weren't easier. I was sturdier. That's the kind of abundance that doesn't fluctuate.

You Live What You Rehearse

Earlier in this chapter, we talked about rehearsal. This is where it becomes especially important. Because in overflow, you are no longer rehearsing for a future life. You are rehearsing how you *live* your current one.

You rehearse

- responding instead of reacting,
- choosing clarity over chaos,

- trusting yourself to adjust,
- honoring your limits without guilt, and
- staying present when things are uncertain.

These rehearsals are subtle. But they are cumulative. And they shape your default state.

Breakthroughs are exciting. They're also unstable if the baseline isn't there to support them. Default mode manifestation is about what happens *between* breakthroughs: How you live on an average Tuesday. How you speak to yourself when no one is watching. How you treat your energy when nothing dramatic is happening.

This is where lives are actually built. Overflow is sustained here.

Releasing the Addiction to Intensity

This is a tender moment for many people. They realize they've been addicted to intensity. Not joy. Intensity. High highs. Low lows. Constant stimulation. Emotional roller coasters. Intensity can feel like purpose when you've lived in survival. Overflow feels flatter at first. Not dull. Stable. And stability can feel boring until your nervous system recalibrates.

Once it does, something beautiful happens. You start noticing subtler pleasures.

Deeper satisfaction. Quieter joy. Joy that doesn't spike and crash. Joy that stays.

At this stage, identity integration becomes key. You are no longer "becoming" someone. You are **living as** someone.

Someone who

- trusts herself,
- responds instead of reacts,
- chooses alignment over approval,
- values progress over perfection, and
- understands growth is ongoing.

This identity doesn't require constant reinforcement. It's reinforced through lived experience. And that makes it resilient.

When Old Voices Resurface

Even in overflow, old voices may surface. The inner critic. The pressure to do more. The fear of losing what you've built. This doesn't mean you've regressed. It means you're human.

The difference now is that you don't obey those voices automatically. You listen. You discern. You choose. That choice is power.

It's important to say this clearly: Living in overflow does not mean controlling your life. It means leading yourself through it.

Leadership includes

- knowing when to act,
- knowing when to wait,
- knowing when to rest, and
- knowing when to stretch.

You don't outsource this authority anymore. You trust yourself. That trust changes how life meets you.

Practice: Noticing Ease Without Sabotage

Try this: The next time something feels easy, notice what arises.

Do you tense?

Do you look for the catch?

Do you rush to fill the space?

Instead of reacting, pause. Say to yourself: "This is allowed." Let your body experience ease without justification. This is nervous system re-education. And it matters more than you think.

Ease is not something you stumble into. It's something you learn to allow. Overflow is not about avoiding effort. It's about releasing unnecessary strain. It's about trusting that you can grow without burning yourself out. That you can expand without abandoning yourself. That you can want more without destabilizing what you have.

One of the most surprising things about living in overflow is how ordinary it feels at first. Not disappointing. Not dull. Just … steady.

There's no dramatic "I made it" moment. No permanent high. No finish line tape snapping across your chest. Instead, there is a subtle shift in how you move through your days.

You wake up without dread. You respond instead of react. You handle problems without spiraling. You recover faster. You trust yourself more. And because we've been conditioned to equate intensity with progress, this steadiness can feel unfamiliar. Sometimes even suspicious.

When Ease Triggers Old Conditioning

For many people, ease is not neutral. It's threatening. Because ease contradicts everything they were taught about worth, safety, and success. If you were raised in environments where love was conditional, rest was earned, or survival required vigilance, your nervous system learned a powerful equation:

Effort equals safety. Strain equals value. Ease equals danger. So, when default mode manifestation begins to take hold and life feels more spacious, the old alarms go off.

"You're getting lazy."

"This won't last."

"You should be doing more."

"Something bad is coming."

These thoughts don't mean you're regressing. They mean your system is learning a new baseline. Overflow requires **re-education**, not discipline.

Living in overflow does not mean you stop working. It means you stop fighting yourself while you work. There is a profound difference between effort and strain.

Effort is clean. It comes from clarity. It feels purposeful. Strain is anxious. It comes from fear. It feels compulsive.

In survival mode, most effort is actually strain. You push because you're afraid of what will happen if you don't. You overproduce to avoid judgment. You overextend to feel worthy.

In overflow, effort remains, but strain dissolves. You still act. You still build. You still show up. But your actions are no longer fueled by self-threat. That shift alone frees up enormous energy.

One of the earliest signs that default mode manifestation is stabilizing is a change in how time feels. Time doesn't slow down. But it stops chasing you.

You're no longer living with an internal metronome screaming,

"You're behind."

"Hurry up."

"You should be further by now."

Urgency is a trauma response. Presence is a regulated state. When urgency loosens, time becomes a collaborator instead of an enemy. You make decisions more cleanly. You stop rushing outcomes. You stop panicking when things unfold more slowly than expected.

And paradoxically, things often move faster. Not because you're pushing, but because you're aligned.

Many people live under invisible internal deadlines they never consciously chose.

"I should have figured this out by now."

"At my age, I should be further."

"If this doesn't happen soon, it never will."

These deadlines create constant low-grade stress. They drain energy quietly and relentlessly. Overflow doesn't erase ambition. It removes **self-punishment**. You still want growth.

You still want expansion. But you're no longer threatening yourself to get there. Progress replaces panic.

Progress Over Perfection

This is one of the most stabilizing principles of overflow: **Progress matters more than perfection.** Perfection is rigid. Progress is adaptive.

Perfection says: "If I can't do it right, I won't do it at all."

Progress says: "I'll adjust as I go."

Living in overflow means you stop using perfection as a reason to stall. You let yourself be human. You repair instead of restarting. You recalibrate instead of quitting. This creates continuity. And continuity is what builds sustainable momentum.

Your life does not become problem-free.

Your **capacity expands**. What once felt overwhelming now feels workable. What once triggered panic now triggers problem-solving. What once knocked you off course now slows you briefly.

This is not because you've numbed yourself. It's because your nervous system has learned resilience. You trust yourself to respond.

That trust is abundance.

Default mode manifestation is built through rehearsal. Not visualization alone. Not intention alone. Rehearsal in daily moments.

You rehearse

- how you speak to yourself when plans change,
- how you respond to discomfort,
- how you treat your energy when no one is watching,
- how you handle mistakes, and
- how quickly you return to center.

These micro-rehearsals install your baseline. Overflow emerges when your default response becomes: "I can handle this."

Breakthroughs are exciting. But they're unstable without a supportive baseline. Many people experience temporary breakthroughs only to regress because their nervous system can't sustain the change. Overflow is not built in peak moments. It's built on ordinary days.

On average Tuesdays. On quiet mornings. On unremarkable decisions. This is where identity solidifies.

Releasing the Addiction to Intensity

Many people are not addicted to pain. They're addicted to **intensity**. Chaos feels familiar. High drama feels alive. Urgency feels productive. Stability can feel flat at first.

Overflow is quieter than survival.

But it's deeper.

As your system recalibrates, you begin to experience joy that doesn't spike and crash.

Satisfaction that doesn't require adrenaline.

Peace that doesn't depend on everything going right. This is nervous system maturity.

At this stage, identity stops being something you work on. It becomes something you live from. You are no longer "becoming" confident. You move as someone who trusts herself. You are no longer "working on abundance." You relate to resources with steadiness. You are no longer "healing to be worthy." You operate from inherent worth.

This integration is subtle. But it's profound.

When Old Voices Resurface

Even in overflow, old voices may appear: The inner critic. The urge to overdo. The fear of losing momentum. This doesn't mean you're failing. It means growth is ongoing. The difference now is discernment. You hear the voice. You don't obey it automatically.

You choose. Choice is overflow in action.

Living in overflow is not about control. It's about leadership. Leadership of your energy. Leadership of your responses. Leadership of your pace.

You know when to move. You know when to pause. You know when to rest. You know when to stretch. You trust your internal authority. And life responds to that trust.

Here's a practice that matters more than it sounds: When something feels easy, let it be easy.

Notice the impulse to

- overthink,
- add pressure,
- create urgency, or
- "earn" the ease.

Pause. Tell your body:
"This is safe."
This is how overflow stabilizes.

Integration: Recognizing Default Mode

Ask yourself:

- How do I handle stress now compared to a year ago?
- How quickly do I recover?

- How much do I trust myself to respond?
- How often do I abandon myself under pressure?

Your answers tell you more than any manifestation metric.

Ease Is Learned

Overflow is not accidental. It is learned.

Learned through repetition. Learned through self-trust. Learned through choosing progress over perfection. Learned through expanding capacity instead of demanding flawlessness.

You are not meant to live at the edge of burnout. You are meant to live from a regulated, responsive center.

There is a moment when you realize you are no longer practicing manifestation. You are living it. Not consciously. Not ceremonially. Not with constant intention-setting or mental checklists. It's happening quietly, in the background of your life:

In how you wake up

In how you respond to stress

In how you make decisions without spiraling

In how you trust yourself to figure things out as you go

That's when you know default mode manifestation has taken root. Not because everything is perfect. But because **you are no longer at war with yourself**.

Most people expect overflow to announce itself with fireworks, a massive breakthrough, a dramatic turning point, a moment they'll tell the story of forever. But more often than not, overflow arrives on an ordinary day:

- Nothing major goes wrong.
- Nothing dramatic goes right.
- And yet … you feel steady.

You handle an inconvenience without losing your center. You receive good news without gripping. You face uncertainty without collapsing. And later, you realize:

"I would not have handled that this way a year ago."

That's overflow. Not the absence of challenge. The presence of capacity.

When Intuition Makes No Sense Until Later

Not all guidance arrives with symbols and ceremony. Sometimes it shows up as a logistical decision that makes no rational sense in the moment. At one retreat, I was assigning roommates.

Skyler was in her twenties. Dionne was in her fifties. On paper, they did not "match." Different life stages. Different backgrounds. Different energies. And yet, when I was placing names into rooms, something in me said: put them together.

There was no argument for it. No pros and cons list. Just a quiet knowing. So, I did. That week, both women ended up doing profound womb healing work. Unrelated on the surface. Deeply connected underneath. They became mirrors for each other. Different generations. Same theme.

One healing forward. One healing backward. Neither of them had come to the retreat expecting that focus. But it unfolded naturally. Organically. As if something had already paired their stories before I ever assigned the room.

Roommates who didn't "make sense." Shared womb healing. Intuition often arrives as a quiet knowing, not a logical argument. It does not demand to be understood in the moment. It simply asks to be trusted. Later, you look back and realize the intelligence that was moving through you. Not because you overanalyzed it. But because you followed it.

This is the truth that quietly replaces the fantasy of arrival: **Who you become matters more than where you end up**.

Destinations change. Circumstances shift. Goals evolve.

But who you are when you meet those changes determines everything. You can manifest the same outcome from two different identities and have two completely different experiences of it. One identity arrives anxious, afraid to lose it, waiting for the other shoe to drop. Another arrives grounded, present, and capable of enjoying what they've created.

Overflow is not about collecting outcomes. It's about becoming someone who can live well inside them.

It softens. Living in overflow does not mean growth ends. It means growth stops feeling violent.

Earlier in life, growth often feels like rupture. Like something must break for something else to be born. In overflow, growth becomes organic.

You still outgrow things. You still release identities. You still stretch. But you do it with self-trust instead of self-threat. Growth stops demanding suffering as proof. It becomes collaborative.

When Life Feels Different Because You Are Different

People will sometimes ask, "What changed?"

And you won't know how to answer.

Because externally, things might look similar. Same responsibilities. Same relationships. Same rhythms. But internally, everything has shifted.

You don't personalize delays. You don't catastrophize discomfort. You don't abandon yourself under pressure. Life feels different because **you are different**. That is the most honest definition of manifestation I know.

Earlier in this chapter, we talked about rehearsal. This is where it lands. Because by now, you're no longer rehearsing for a future version of yourself. You're rehearsing **how you live**.

You rehearse

- staying present when plans shift,
- responding instead of reacting,
- choosing integrity over urgency,
- honoring your energy instead of overriding it, and
- trusting yourself to adjust.

These rehearsals have become automatic. And automation is what makes overflow sustainable.

At this stage, progress over perfection is no longer a concept. It's how you move.

You don't wait to be flawless.

You don't scrap the whole plan because one day went sideways.

You don't use mistakes as evidence that you're failing.

You course correct. You repair. You continue. This creates momentum that doesn't burn you out. And burnout is one of the greatest blocks to overflow.

Problems Still Arise

You just don't collapse into them. Let's be honest. Life will continue to present problems.

There will still be

- unexpected expenses,
- uncomfortable conversations,
- disappointments,
- detours, and
- moments of doubt.

Overflow does not remove these. It changes how much **power** they have over you. Problems become events, not identities. Challenges become information, not threats. You respond from capacity instead of panic. And that changes outcomes more than people realize.

One of the most noticeable shifts in default mode manifestation is confidence that doesn't need to be announced. You stop explaining yourself. You stop seeking constant reassurance. You stop over-preparing for rejection. You trust your discernment.

That trust shows up in your body. In your tone. In your pacing. In your boundaries. People feel it. Not as dominance. As steadiness. And steadiness is magnetic.

It's honest presence. There's a misconception that living in overflow means being endlessly grateful, positive, or serene. It doesn't.

Overflow includes

- frustration without self-attack,
- sadness without despair,
- anger without destruction, and
- joy without clinging.

You experience the full spectrum of being human. But you no longer believe every emotion means something is wrong. You let feelings move. You don't build identities around them. This emotional literacy is part of mastery.

When Old Patterns Try to Re-enter

Even in overflow, old patterns may knock: The urge to rush. The desire to overgive.

The temptation arises to abandon your own rhythm to meet external expectations. The difference now is awareness. You recognize the pattern. You pause. You choose differently. That pause is not hesitation. It's sovereignty.

At some point, you stop measuring your life by individual manifestations. You start measuring it by **quality of experience**.

How often do you feel present?

How deeply do you trust yourself?

How quickly do you recover?

How honest are you with yourself?

How aligned do your choices feel?

This is when manifestation stops being transactional. It becomes relational. A relationship with life. With yourself. With uncertainty. And that relationship is what creates sustained abundance.

Overflow is not something you "enter" and then try to maintain. It's something you live into, day by day. Some days feel expansive. Some days feel quiet. Some days feel challenging.

But your baseline remains intact. You don't collapse. You don't self-abandon. You don't lose yourself. That consistency is the real win.

PRACTICE

Instead of asking, "What am I manifesting?"

Ask: "How am I living?"

Notice the following:

- How do you speak to yourself?
- How do you respond to stress?
- How do you treat your energy?
- How do you make decisions?

These are your true manifestation metrics. And if you're honest, you'll see how far you've come.

Closing: You Are Already Living It

Here is what I want you to know as you close this chapter, and this phase of the work: You are not waiting to live in overflow. You are already doing it in ways you may not yet recognize.

It happens every time you choose progress over perfection. Every time you respond instead of react. Every time you trust yourself to adjust. Every time you stay present without forcing outcomes.

That is default mode manifestation. Not magic. Not fantasy. Not arrival.

Life, lived from coherence. You don't need to chase overflow. You need to **continue living from the version of you that already knows how to hold life**. That version is here. And from here, everything else unfolds naturally.

Reflection Questions

Take time with these questions:

1. Where in my life do I feel most grounded right now?
2. How has my response to stress changed?
3. What no longer triggers me the way it used to?
4. Where do I trust myself more than I once did?
5. What does overflow look like in my *actual* life?

Write without performance.
This chapter is about embodiment, not aspiration.

CHAPTER 11

Pivot or Persist: How to Trust Yourself Through Every Season

There comes a moment in every life when the question changes.

Not *"What do I want?"*

Not *"How do I manifest it?"*

Not even *"Why isn't this working yet?"*

The question becomes quieter and more personal. *"Do I keep going … or do I choose again?"*

This question doesn't usually arrive during chaos. It arrives during stability. When things are "fine." When progress exists, but excitement doesn't. When you've invested time, energy, identity … and something inside you has shifted. This is the moment most people mishandle.

Not because they lack intuition. But because they've been taught that changing direction means failure. So, they stay. They persist past alignment. They push past resonance. They keep going long after the season has changed.

Not out of devotion. Out of fear.

Up until now, this book has taught you how to align.

- How to regulate your nervous system.
- How to work with identity.
- How to take aligned action.
- How to surrender without stalling.
- How to live in overflow as a baseline state.

But none of that matters if you don't trust yourself when the path *changes*. Because manifestation mastery is not about staying on one road forever. It's about knowing when to **persist** and when to **pivot**, without outsourcing your authority, abandoning yourself, or rewriting history as regret. This chapter is not about motivation. It's about discernment.

The Lie That Keeps People Stuck

There is a lie that sounds like responsibility.

It says:

"You've already invested so much."

"You can't quit now."

"Just push through."

"Everyone feels this way."

"This is what commitment looks like."

But here's the truth most people never hear: **Commitment to a path is not the same as commitment to yourself.** You can be loyal to something that no longer fits. You can persist past the point of truth. You can confuse endurance with integrity.

And when you do, doubt creeps in, not because you're weak, but because your intuition is being ignored.

Doubt is often framed as the enemy. Something to overcome. But doubt isn't always the problem. Unexamined doubt is. Because doubt doesn't always mean *"stop."*

Sometimes it means:

"Something here has changed."

"You are not the same person who started this."

"There is more information now."

"This path needs updating."

Doubt becomes a thief of dreams only when it's left unconscious. When you ignore it, suppress it, or shame yourself for feeling it, doubt grows louder. But when you listen to it without panic, it becomes discernment.

One of the most dangerous assumptions in personal growth is the idea that alignment is static. That once something is "right," it should always be right. But life doesn't work that way.

You change. Your nervous system evolves. Your capacity expands. Your values refine.

What once felt expansive may now feel restrictive.

What once required courage may now require release.

What once was aligned may now be complete.

Completion is not failure. Completion is *honoring timing*.

There was a time in my life when I stayed in a friendship that had already taught me everything it could.

It wasn't terrible. It wasn't wrong. It just wasn't alive anymore.

Externally, it still made sense. Internally, something had gone quiet. But I didn't trust that quiet.

I stayed. I justified. I pushed. I told myself commitment meant endurance. What I didn't realize then was that my intuition wasn't trying to sabotage me. It was trying to free me.

When I finally chose differently, I didn't feel relief right away. I felt grief. Not because I failed. But because I honored what was ending. That grief was clean. And on the other side of it was clarity I couldn't have accessed any other way.

The Difference Between Fear and Completion

One of the hardest skills to develop is distinguishing fear from completion.

Fear feels loud.

Urgent.

Panicked.

Completion feels quiet.

Resolved.

Clear.

Fear says:

"What if you're wrong?"

"What if you regret this?"

"What if this was your only chance?"

Completion says:

"This chapter has given what it needed to give."

"You are not abandoning yourself by moving on."

"Trust the version of you that sees further."

Fear wants certainty.
Completion offers peace.
Learning to tell the difference changes your life.

Let's be clear: persistence is not the villain. There are seasons where persistence is sacred, where things feel hard not because they're wrong, but because they're stretching you, where discomfort is growth, not misalignment. So how do you know the difference?

Persistence that is aligned:

- Feels challenging but purposeful
- Stretches you without shrinking you
- Asks for courage, not self-abandonment
- Still feels alive beneath the effort

Persistence that is misaligned:

- Feels heavy and numbing
- Requires constant justification
- Drains your energy without renewal
- Silences your intuition instead of strengthening it

This is not a logic problem. It's a **body truth**.

Pivoting Isn't Failure

We need to say this plainly and without apology: **Pivoting is not failure.** Pivoting is responsiveness.

It's what intelligent systems do.
It's what living organisms do.
It's what growth requires.

Failure is staying loyal to an identity that no longer fits because you're afraid to be seen as inconsistent. Pivoting requires more courage than persisting blindly.

Because it asks you to release

- certainty,
- familiarity,
- external validation, and
- the story of who you thought you were.

That's not weakness. That's evolution.

There is a version of courage that doesn't look like grit. It looks like honesty.

It looks like saying:

"This isn't aligned anymore."

"I've changed."

"I'm allowed to choose again."

Courage is not sticking it out no matter what. Courage is choosing again **from truth**, not fear. And you don't need permission to do that.

This phrase is one of the most powerful reclaims of sovereignty you can make.

That was then. This is now.

It doesn't erase the past. It doesn't invalidate what you learned. It doesn't mean you were wrong.

It means you are present. It means you're not forcing continuity where evolution is required. This is how you stop rewriting your past as a mistake. You let it be a chapter. And then you turn the page consciously.

Indecision has a cost. Staying in limbo drains energy. Overanalyzing erodes trust.

Waiting for certainty keeps you dependent. When you don't choose, something else chooses for you.

Circumstances.

Resentment.

Burnout.

Disconnection.

Choosing, even imperfectly, restores power.

The you who started this journey was brave. But the you who is reading this now has more information.

More experience. More capacity.

It's time to trust *that* version. Not the one who was afraid to begin.

The one who has walked far enough to see the landscape differently.

Growth grants perspective. Perspective grants authority.

This Is a Discernment Chapter

This chapter is not asking you to quit. And it's not asking you to push.

It's asking you to **listen**.

To recognize that seasons change. That alignment evolves. That self-trust is built by choosing consciously, not clinging unconsciously. There is a moment, usually quiet, when you realize that the question is no longer *whether* you can keep going.

The question is whether you **should**.

Not because you're incapable.

Not because you're tired.

Not because you're failing.

But because something in you has changed. And that realization can feel destabilizing if you don't understand what's happening because we are taught to celebrate beginnings. To praise perseverance. To admire endurance. But we are rarely taught how to **end things well**.

Most people are not afraid of making the wrong choice. They're afraid of being wrong *about themselves.*

They fear

- misreading intuition,
- confusing fear with truth,
- regretting a decision they can't undo,
- disappointing people who believed in them, and
- invalidating their past effort.

So instead of choosing, they stall. They stay in analysis. They wait for certainty. They look for external confirmation. They ask for signs, reassurance, permission. And slowly, without realizing it, they outsource their authority. This is how people become dependent on frameworks instead of being embodied in wisdom. Let's undo that.

One of the most important truths about pivoting or persisting is this: **You are never deciding in a vacuum.** Your body has been sending signals for a long time. You just haven't been taught how to read them without panic.

Signals of misalignment often show up as the following:

- Chronic exhaustion that rest doesn't fix
- Resentment toward things you once loved
- Fantasizing about escape rather than expansion
- A sense of obligation without inspiration
- Increased irritability or numbness
- Procrastination that feels protective, not lazy

Signals of alignment under pressure look different:

- Fear paired with excitement
- Fatigue that lifts once you begin
- Resistance that softens after movement
- Challenge that sharpens rather than dulls you
- Discomfort that feels purposeful

These signals are not abstract. They are embodied information.

Guilt is one of the biggest distorters of intuition, especially guilt tied to

- sunk cost,
- loyalty,
- identity, or
- expectation.

"I can't quit now."

"People are counting on me."

"I've already put so much into this."

"This is who I said I was."

Guilt keeps you loyal to the *past version* of yourself. Discernment asks you to honor the present one. This is why pivoting feels selfish to people who have never been taught sovereignty. But self-betrayal is not generosity. It's slow erosion.

Let's talk about sunk cost honestly. Just because you invested time, money, or identity into something does not mean you owe it your future. Sunk cost thinking sounds noble. But it often disguises fear.

Fear of

- wasted effort,
- embarrassment,
- starting over, or
- admitting change.

Here is the truth that liberates people: **Nothing that taught you something was wasted.** Completion is not erasure. You don't need to keep paying for a lesson once it's been learned.

When Persistence Becomes Self-abandonment

Persistence is often praised as strength. But persistence without alignment becomes self-abandonment.

You know this is happening when

- you override your body repeatedly;
- you minimize your own needs;
- you tell yourself "it's not that bad" daily;
- you fantasize about relief more than growth; or
- you feel trapped by your own commitments.

At that point, continuing is no longer noble. It's numbing. And numbing is not spiritual maturity.

One of the deepest fears around pivoting is relational.

"What will people think?"

"They'll say I can't stick with anything."

"They'll lose respect for me."

"I'll look flaky."

This fear keeps people in identities they've already outgrown. But here's the truth most people don't say out loud: people who are threatened by your evolution were benefiting from your stagnation. The people who respect you will understand. And the people who don't, they were never meant to define you.

The you who started this path had limited information. The you who is reading this now has lived experience. You have walked far enough to see around corners you couldn't see before. So why would you hold yourself to a decision made from an earlier vantage point?

Growth gives you new sight. New sight gives you new responsibility. That responsibility is to trust the version of you who sees further.

I remember a moment when I realized I was no longer who I had been when I made a certain commitment. At first, I thought something was wrong with me.

Why couldn't I just push through?

Why did it suddenly feel heavy?

Why was my enthusiasm gone?

Then I asked a different question. "What if this chapter is complete?" That question didn't bring immediate relief. It brought grief. Because ending something consciously requires honoring what it gave you. But once I allowed that grief, clarity followed. And clarity brought clean action.

Not reaction. Not escape. Choice.

Courage Is Choosing Again (Without Burning the Bridge)

Courage is not reckless pivoting. It's conscious choosing. Sometimes courage looks like staying. Sometimes it looks like leaving. Sometimes it looks like redefining the terms.

Pivoting doesn't mean burning everything down.

It can mean

- renegotiating boundaries,
- changing pace,
- shifting roles,
- redefining success, or
- allowing something to evolve.

Pivoting with integrity preserves your self-respect.

Here's something most people need to hear: you will never have 100% certainty. If you wait for certainty, you will wait forever. Discernment does not require certainty.

It requires honesty.

Ask:

- Which option expands me, even if it scares me?
- Which option preserves comfort but dulls my aliveness?
- Which choice would future-me respect?

Your body will answer before your mind does.

When you don't choose,

- resentment builds,
- energy drains,
- creativity stalls, and
- intuition dulls.

Not choosing keeps you dependent on circumstances instead of on self-trust. Choosing, even imperfectly, reclaims authority.

Once you choose, move forward cleanly, no mental back-tracking, no self-shaming, no rewriting history as failure.

You didn't "quit." You completed.

You didn't "give up." You grew.

You didn't "lose time." You gained wisdom.

Language matters here. Your subconscious is listening.

Integration Practice: The Discernment Check

Take out your journal and answer honestly:

- What feels complete, even if I'm afraid to admit it?
- What still feels alive, even if it's uncomfortable?
- Where am I persisting out of fear rather than truth?
- Where am I ready to choose again?

Sit with the answers. No urgency. No pressure. Truth doesn't need force.

By now, something should feel clearer.

Not resolved. But quieter.

Discernment doesn't shout. It settles. This part of the chapter is not meant to push you toward a decision. It's meant to reconnect you with your **internal authority**. There is a moment when self-trust stops being something you practice and becomes something you **stand on**.

It doesn't feel dramatic.

It doesn't arrive with fireworks.

It doesn't announce itself loudly.

It feels like a quiet internal click.

A moment where you realize:

"I don't need to keep asking."

"I don't need more proof."

"I don't need permission."

That moment is not the end of the journey. It's the moment you stop outsourcing your authority. And that is what this chapter is really about.

Doubt is often described as fear. But in its most corrosive form, doubt is something subtler.

It is the voice that says:

"You can't trust yourself."

"You need more time."

"You need someone else to confirm this."

"You're probably misreading things."

This is why doubt is a thief of dreams. Not because it questions outcomes. But because it questions *you*. And once you doubt your ability to decide, you give your power away—to people, systems, timing, circumstances, or fear itself. The final work of this chapter is not eliminating doubt. It's **removing doubt's authority**.

Everything you've learned in this book ultimately points here. Thought work matters.

Emotional regulation matters. Identity matters. Action matters. Surrender matters. But none of it holds if you don't trust yourself when things get ambiguous because life will always include ambiguity.

There will always be moments when

- the path isn't clear,
- the results aren't immediate,
- the choice feels risky, and
- the future is undefined.

In those moments, self-trust is what keeps you moving without forcing, collapsing, or numbing. Self-trust is what allows manifestation to remain embodied instead of performative.

Choosing Again Is Not Inconsistency

It's conscious evolution. One of the biggest lies people carry is that consistency means staying the same. It doesn't. Consistency means staying aligned with truth as it evolves. Choosing again does not mean you were wrong before. It means you are honest now.

Pivoting is not failure. It is responsiveness.

Life is not linear. Growth is not static. Identity is not fixed. If you insist on staying who you were to prove reliability, you sacrifice authenticity. And authenticity is the foundation of sustainable success, love, and fulfillment.

Let's redefine courage one last time:

Courage is not pushing through at all costs.

Courage is not endurance for endurance's sake.

Courage is not loyalty to outdated versions of yourself.

Courage is choosing again when the old choice no longer reflects who you are.

Courage is saying:

"This worked for me then."

"This is no longer aligned now."

"I trust myself to choose again."

That kind of courage doesn't look impressive from the outside. But it feels solid on the inside. And solidity is what holds you when things change.

"That Was Then. This Is Now."

This phrase is not a dismissal of your past. It is a **blessing** of it.

That was then.

This is now.

That was the version of you who needed that lesson. This is the version of you who carries it forward.

When you use this phrase consciously, something powerful happens.

You stop arguing with your history.

You stop defending old decisions.

You stop proving continuity where evolution is required.

You allow chapters to close cleanly.

And clean endings create clean beginnings.

Declaring the New Chapter Consciously

One of the reasons people feel stuck between pivot and persist is because they never *declare* the transition.

They drift.

They fade.

They half-leave.

They stay mentally attached to what they've already outgrown.

This creates energetic leakage. Conscious declaration seals identity.

It doesn't require a public announcement.

It doesn't require explanation.

It requires **internal clarity**.

A quiet, embodied decision:

"This chapter is complete."

"I am choosing differently now."

"I trust this choice."

When you declare internally, your nervous system stabilizes. And when your nervous system stabilizes, action follows naturally.

The you who started this book needed guidance. The you who is finishing it needs **permission to lead herself**. You have walked far enough to see patterns. To recognize cycles. To notice what drains you and what feeds you. To feel the difference between fear and truth. That perspective matters.

Do not hand decision-making power back to the version of you who hadn't yet lived this.

Honor her.

Thank her.

But trust the one who sees further.

That is maturity.

Many people stay stuck because they fear regret.

"What if I regret leaving?"

"What if I regret staying?"

"What if I choose wrong?"

Here is something deeply grounding:

Regret does not come from choosing.

It comes from **abandoning yourself while choosing**. You can make a choice that doesn't work out and still trust yourself.

You can pivot and learn.

You can persist and adjust.

What creates regret is staying silent when you knew better.

Listening to yourself, even when the outcome is uncertain, builds self-respect. And self-respect dissolves regret.

Living Beyond Binary Thinking

Pivot or persist is not always a binary choice.

Sometimes it's

- persist, but differently;
- pivot internally before pivoting externally;
- persist in purpose, pivot in form;
- stay, but renegotiate terms; or
- leave slowly, with integration.

Self-trust allows nuance.

You stop asking, "What's the right answer?"

And start asking, "What's the most honest one?"

Honesty is always the compass.

There was a moment in my life when I realized I had been asking the wrong question.

I kept asking: "What should I do?"

Instead of: "Who am I now?"

When I answered the second question, the first answered itself.

The decision wasn't easy.

But it was clean.

And clean decisions don't haunt you.

They anchor you.

This is the part where many books subtly keep the reader hooked.

They imply:

"You'll need more tools."

"You'll need ongoing guidance."

"You'll need someone to tell you what to do next."

This book is not doing that because the goal of this work is **self-sovereignty**.

You are not meant to depend on methods forever.

You are meant to embody discernment.

If you have learned anything here, let it be this:

You can trust yourself through uncertainty.

You can trust yourself through change.

You can trust yourself even when you don't have all the answers.

Especially then.

Self-trust is not a one-time achievement. It's a relationship that you strengthen every time you

- listen to your body,
- honor your intuition,

- choose alignment over approval,
- respond instead of react, or
- tell yourself the truth.

Over time, this relationship becomes unshakeable.

Not because life gets easier.

But because you stop doubting your capacity to meet it.

Practice: Declaring the Chapter

Take a moment with your journal. Write this sentence and finish it honestly: "The chapter of my life that is complete is …" Then write:

"The chapter I am consciously choosing now is …"

Don't rush.

Don't perform.

Don't justify.

This is between you and yourself. Seal it.

Signs, Synchronicities, and Guidance (Listening Without Losing Yourself)

THE QUIET POWER OF STAYING WITH YOURSELF

Perhaps the most radical part of this method is that it teaches you how to stay with yourself when things feel uncertain. No bypassing. No abandoning. No numbing.

Just presence. And presence is magnetic.

WHY YOU DON'T NEED TO KNOW THE PATH

One of the most liberating truths in manifestation is this: You do not need to see the whole path.

You need to stay in motion. Clarity follows commitment.

There was a woman named Miriam who wanted a new career but couldn't see how it would happen. During the method, she released limiting beliefs, continued applying, and trusted the process.

Eventually, she landed her dream job. Not because she knew how. But because she kept going.

Manifestation responds to **movement**, not certainty.

LISTENING WITHOUT LOSING YOURSELF

There is a phase in manifestation work that is rarely talked about clearly.

After resistance softens.

After self-trust stabilizes.

After overflow becomes your baseline.

Something subtle begins to happen. You start noticing more. Not because the universe suddenly got louder. But because you did.

You notice timing that feels precise.

Encounters that feel aligned.

Symbols that appear at threshold moments.

Conversations that answer questions you haven't spoken aloud.

And the question becomes: Are these signs?

Or am I projecting meaning onto randomness? This is where many people either spiral into magical thinking or shut themselves down completely.

This chapter is about neither. It's about discernment.

Some Moments Are Meant to Be Lived

There are times when symbols repeat. And then there are moments that feel so precise you almost don't want to talk about them because they sound made up.

One afternoon at retreat, Dionne and I were walking together. She had just shared something vulnerable about her voice. About how she had hidden it for years. About how singing felt both sacred and terrifying.

Her voice is a gift. Clear. Warm. Resonant. But like many women, she had learned to quiet it. We were holding hands when it happened. A black bird with a bright orange puff on its chest landed nearby.

And I froze because Dionne was wearing black with a bright orange wrap across her chest. The markings were nearly identical. The bird perched close. Not startled. Not frantic. Just present. And then it began to sing. Not a random chirp. A melody.

Dionne laughed in disbelief and softly sang back. The bird responded. Back and forth. Call and response. Harmony. It felt like witnessing a duet that had been waiting to happen. We both just stood there, hands still clasped, listening. When the bird finally flew off, she turned to me and said, "I'm glad you were here because nobody would believe me." That line stayed with me.

Some moments aren't meant to be proven. They're meant to be lived. Was it a message? Was it coincidence? Was it nature doing what nature does? Maybe all of it. But here is what I know: She had been reclaiming her voice all week. And in that moment, something in the natural world mirrored it back to her.

Not as instruction. As resonance. The Universe often speaks through nature, through rhythm, through reflection. Not to convince you. But to affirm what is already awakening inside you.

Not everything is a sign. And not everything is random.

A signal is not superstition.

It is not a fortune prediction.

It is not proof that you're "chosen."

A signal has three qualities:

1. **It appears at a threshold moment**.
2. **It carries internal resonance**.
3. **It often repeats**.

A signal interrupts your awareness in a meaningful way.

It does not demand panic.

It does not require dramatization.

It does not override your agency.

It sharpens it. A symbol is not a fortune teller. It is a marker. And sometimes, markers appear exactly when you are crossing into something new.

The moment a sign tells you what to do instead of helping you clarify what you already know, you have crossed into outsourcing. Mature guidance feels like confirmation, not coercion.

It strengthens your discernment. It does not replace it. If a symbol creates urgency, panic, or dependency, pause. If it creates clarity, steadiness, or quiet alignment, listen. Guidance does not override your nervous system regulation; it works in partnership with it.

The Interpretation Rules

Before assigning meaning to anything, run it through these filters:

1. **Check Your Emotional State**

   Were you regulated or dysregulated when you noticed it?

   A calm nervous system interprets clearly.

   A dysregulated one seeks control.

   Never interpret from panic.

2. **Look for Repetition**

   One random event is just that.

   Two or three aligned repetitions at threshold moments deserve attention.

   Repetition reduces projection.

3. **Separate Symbol from Story**

   The symbol is neutral.

   Your story is optional.

   Example:

   A bird hits a window.

   Symbol: interruption.

   Story: "This means disaster is coming."

   One is observation.

   One is fear.

   Stay with observation.

4. **Ask: Does This Increase Responsibility or Avoid It?**

   Real guidance increases accountability.

   It does not excuse passivity.

   If your "sign" allows you to avoid a difficult conversation, delay action, or blame fate, it is not guidance. It is avoidance.

5. **Notice the Aftereffect**

   True signals increase presence.

   They do not create obsession.

   If you find yourself compulsively searching for more confirmation, step back.

   Alignment is steady.

   Anxiety is hungry.

Synchronicity Is Coherence, Not Control

Synchronicities increase when your internal world is coherent. When thought, emotion, and action align, life often feels responsive. But responsiveness does not mean the universe is a vending machine. It means you are congruent.

And congruence sharpens perception. You begin noticing doors because you are finally walking toward them. You begin noticing people because you are finally clear about what you value. You begin noticing symbols because you are finally present enough to see them. Synchronicity is not magic; it is alignment meeting opportunity.

When Nothing Happens

There will be seasons where signs feel obvious. And seasons where everything feels quiet. Quiet is not abandonment. Quiet is integration. Do not create drama to feel connected. Do not manufacture intensity to feel guided. Guidance is subtle more often than it is cinematic. And maturity means trusting yourself even when the sky is silent.

Living with Guidance Without Losing Yourself

The goal is not to interpret everything. The goal is to stay attuned.

Attuned to your body.

Attuned to your values.

Attuned to the direction your life is naturally unfolding.

When a signal appears, ask:

What is this inviting me to notice?

What threshold am I standing at?

What would alignment look like here?

Then act from discernment, not superstition.

Sometimes the Sign Isn't for Everyone

There are moments when guidance feels collective. And then there are moments when it feels … assigned. Let me tell you about two.

The first happened during a cacao ceremony at retreat. If you've ever been in a ceremony, you know there is a rhythm to it. A current. A felt sense of where the story is going. That night, a healer named India, from the BriBri tribe, was sharing a teaching about cacao, about heart opening, about ancestral memory.

And suddenly, a bat began circling the space. Now, if you're reading this from a purely logical standpoint, yes, we were in Costa Rica. Bats exist there. This is not shocking.

But what was unusual was the timing. The moment the bat entered, the energy in the room shifted. Not in fear. In alertness. It felt like punctuation. Like something invisible had raised its hand.

Instantly, India knew that the story she was telling needed to change. Instead of continuing the polished, planned explanation, she spoke about shadow. About rebirth. About navigating the unseen. About the parts of ourselves that only come alive in the dark.

The entire ceremony deepened. The bat circled once more and left. And the women in that room felt it. The moment had been redirected. Guidance isn't always dramatic. Sometimes it's responsive. Sometimes it says, "Turn here instead."

The second moment was different. During a sound bath later that week, everyone was lying down in deep meditation. Breathing slowly. Bodies open. Nervous systems softened.

And again, a bat entered the room. This time it didn't circle.

It was accidentally struck by a ceiling fan blade and dropped with a thud. It just so happened that it landed directly on Yvonne's chest. She let it sit with her for a while and then calmly scooped it up and helped it along its way.

Yvonne had been doing the deepest identity work of anyone that week. She had been shedding an old version of herself in real time. Releasing patterns. Breaking agreements. Stepping into a new frequency. In many traditions, bats symbolize rebirth. Death of the old self. Initiation.

It didn't land randomly in a room full of twenty women. It landed on the one woman in active transformation with a history of bat rehabilitation. And I was positioned to witness it. Sometimes the sign isn't for everyone.

Sometimes it's assigned. Sometimes guidance is collective. And sometimes it is precise. And when something precise happens, your job is not to create mythology around it. Your job is to notice it.

Practice

Reflect:

Where have I mistaken anxiety for intuition?

Where have I dismissed quiet clarity because it wasn't dramatic?

What patterns repeat at my own thresholds?

Do signs make me more grounded or more reactive?

Where can I trust myself more deeply?

Write honestly. This chapter is not about believing more. It is about listening better.

Closing: You Leave Here Self-led

You are not meant to be led by symbols. You are meant to be strengthened by awareness. A symbol can mark a threshold. It cannot walk through it for you. Signs do not control your destiny. Your alignment does. And when you are regulated, grounded, and coherent, life begins to feel responsive in ways that are unmistakable. Not because you are chasing magic. But because you are finally living in partnership with reality.

This is where the book releases you. Not because the work is over. But because the authority is now yours.

You don't need certainty.

You don't need guarantees.

You don't need permission.

You need honesty. Presence.

And courage, the quiet kind.

That was then. This is now. And the version of you reading this knows exactly what that means.

Trust her. She will not lead you wrong.

Reflection Questions

Sit with these questions:

1. Where am I being asked to trust myself more deeply?
2. What decision have I been postponing out of fear?
3. What would it look like to choose again without shame?
4. Where have I already outgrown an old identity?
5. What does sovereignty feel like in my body?

Your answers are not instructions. They are confirmations.

Epilogue

There is a moment, usually after the last page, when the noise goes quiet.

It is the kind of stillness where you don't feel rushed to do anything with what you've just read.

The kind where something has already landed. If you're here now, sitting with this book closed or nearly closed, I want you to know something important:

Nothing is missing. Not another technique. Not another lesson. Not another version of you.

You didn't come to this book to be fixed. You came to remember.

The Myth of "One Day"

So many people live their lives waiting for a future version of themselves to arrive.

The confident one. The healed one. The successful one. The peaceful one.

They think,

"One day, when I've done enough work, I'll finally feel settled."

"One day, when things line up, I'll trust myself."

"One day, I'll stop second-guessing."

But there's a quiet truth this work has been pointing toward the entire time.

THAT FUTURE VERSION OF YOU ISN'T COMING. SHE'S ALREADY HERE

She's been here in the moments you chose differently.

In the times you paused instead of panicked.

In the decisions you made without needing approval.

In the days you trusted yourself enough to keep going without proof.

You weren't waiting for the universe. The universe was responding to you.

If you're wondering what changed over the course of this book, the answer is not your circumstances. Some things may have shifted externally. Some things may still be unfolding.

But the real shift happened internally.

You stopped treating yourself like a problem to solve.

You stopped outsourcing your authority.

You stopped believing that alignment required perfection.

You stopped thinking manifestation was something you *did* instead of something you *lived*.

You learned how to listen.

How to regulate.

How to choose.

How to trust.

How to return to yourself again and again.

That is not small. That is mastery.

The End of Chasing

One of the most subtle transformations this work creates is the end of chasing. The frantic energy of trying to get somewhere else to feel okay. The belief that fulfillment lives just beyond your current reach. The habit of constantly preparing for life instead of living it.

You don't need to chase alignment.

You don't need to chase abundance.

You don't need to chase the next version of yourself.

You learned how to *be* where you are without collapsing. And from that place, movement becomes natural. That's the paradox. When you stop chasing, things meet you.

Let's be clear and honest. Life will continue to surprise you. To challenge you. To stretch you.

There will still be moments of uncertainty. Moments of doubt. Moments where old patterns knock at the door. But now, you know how to respond.

You know how to come back to your body. How to check your energy. How to notice when fear is driving. How to pause. How to choose again. You don't need to eliminate struggle to live well. You need to trust yourself inside it. And you do.

If there is one thread that runs through this entire book, it's this: you live what you rehearse.

Not once.

Not perfectly.

But repeatedly.

You rehearsed safety.

You rehearsed self-trust.

You rehearsed aligned action.

You rehearsed regulation instead of reaction.

You rehearsed progress over perfection.

Those rehearsals didn't just change your mindset. They changed your baseline. And baseline is destiny.

This Is Not the End

This is not an ending that asks you to do more. It's an ending that invites you to **live**.

To take what you've integrated and let it move through your days quietly.

To notice how you respond differently now.

To recognize how often you already embody what you once wished for.

You don't need to reread this book constantly.

You don't need to memorize it.

You don't need to hold it tightly.

You can let it sit on a shelf knowing the work has already moved into you. That's how you know it worked.

I want to leave you with this, not as advice, but as recognition:

You were never behind.

You were never broken.

You were never doing it wrong.

You were becoming. And you still are. But now, you're doing it on purpose.

Ask yourself: "How would I live today if I fully trusted myself?"

Then do one small thing from that place. That's it.

Thank you for walking this path with me. As a sovereign creator remembering her own rhythm, you don't need the universe to catch up. It already has.

Acknowledgments

To the woman holding this book,

Thank you for choosing yourself. Thank you for being open, curious, and willing to grow. This work only exists because women like you are ready for something more.

To my A-Team,

Amma, Adam, Avani, Aru, and Ayli.

You are my greatest manifestation and my deepest source of love. Everything I create is rooted in the life we are building together.

To the women who have trusted me, in retreats, in programs, in quiet conversations, and in powerful breakthroughs, you have shaped this work in ways you may never fully realize. Your stories, your courage, your willingness to look within, you are woven into every page of this book.

To my team and the people behind the scenes, thank you for holding space for this vision and helping bring it to life.

To my editor and everyone who helped refine these words, thank you for your care, your precision, and your belief in this message.

And to the version of me who chose this path, who walked away from what was expected, who trusted something she could not fully explain yet, thank you for not turning back.

This book was not created from theory. It was created from lived experience, from witnessing transformation, and from a deep knowing that there is more available to all of us.

And finally, to life, to timing, to the unseen support that meets us when we choose ourselves, thank you.

About the Author

Latha Jay is an author, retreat host, and spiritual guide known for helping women bridge the gap between where they are and who they know they're meant to become.

Blending principles from neuroscience, manifestation, and lived experience, her work focuses on one core truth: transformation does not happen in isolated moments; it happens in the way you think, feel, and show up every day.

Latha's journey began when she made the decision to walk away from the path she had worked so hard to build in medical school, choosing instead to follow a deeper knowing that her work was meant to look different. That decision became the foundation for everything she now teaches: trusting yourself, even when it doesn't make sense yet.

Through her retreats, programs, and online platforms, Latha has supported thousands of women in releasing self-sabotage, reconnecting with their authentic selves, and creating aligned, sustainable change in their lives.

She is also known for creating informative, accessible videos that break down complex concepts around manifestation, mindset, and the nervous system into practical tools people can apply in their everyday lives. Her content reaches millions each month, resonating with those who are ready to stop waiting and start becoming.

Latha is the founder of the **Institute for Conscious Creation**, a space dedicated to bridging science, spirituality, and self-development in a way that is both grounded and transformative.

Latha's work is grounded, honest, and deeply human. She teaches in a way that is both accessible and transformative, helping people understand not just what to do, but how to actually live it.

You can connect with her, learn more about her work, and access her programs and retreats at:

Website: www.lathajay.com

Instagram/TikTok: @latha_jay_

If this book resonated with you, you are not meant to do this work alone. There are spaces, experiences, and communities designed to support you as you continue becoming, where manifestation becomes the way you live, not just something you try.

Index